To JEAN WITH C

LARRY CUMM

KNOCK

When Jesus taught us the Our Father, he said ... 'deliver us from evil'

However,

'The battle against the devil, which is the principal task of Saint Michael the Archangel, is still being fought today, because the devil is still alive and active in the world. The evil that surrounds us today, the disorders that plague our society, man's inconsistency and brokenness, are not only the results of original sin, but also the result of Satan's pervasive and dark action.' John Paul II[1]

but,

'If Jesus is bigger than the Empire State Building, in terms of power, strength & influence, the devil is in comparison the size and strength of a little stinging ant' – 'Anne', A Lay Apostle[2]

Therefore have no fear because

'The power of prayer has overcome enemies (Psalm 6:9-10), as 'nothing is impossible to God'. (Luke 1:37)

Foreword

As the "Age of God's Mercy" on this world of ours is coming to an end and the "Age of God's Justice" is to begin, the Holy Spirit is working overtime to raise up many lay people and priests who have been given a special vocation to bring the mercy and forgiveness of the Heavenly Father to this modern world of ours, which has gone so far away from God.

At the same time, Satan, that age-old enemy of mankind, is also working overtime to seduce and deceive peoples in all kinds of ways. He (Satan) has also many helpers in his evil of drawing people away from God. Satan knows that his time is short and so he, and his evil agents, are hard at work to deceive and capture souls for hell.

Larry Cummins is one of those people whom God in his love and mercy has raised up to counteract the deceptions of this evil.

In this, his second book, he relates for his reader many instances of evil and the disastrous effects they have on a whole range of people both in Ireland and abroad.

Larry is a family man of deep faith and great prayers but is also very humble. He has helped many people discern and overcome their various spiritual problems and difficulties.

This book will serve to enlighten people to understand and discern the root cause of their various spiritual and indeed physical problems and help them find the solution.

I hope and pray that this book will be widely circulated and read by a great number of people who will find it enlightening and bring them back to full physical and spiritual health and given them peace and tranquillity in their lives.

June 24th 2011 – Feast of the Birthday of John the Baptist

Fr. Kevin A. Smith O.Praem,
Holy Trinity Abbey, Kilnacrott, Ballyjamesduff, Co Cavan

Contents

The Reason for this Book

It is Gods ultimate desire that we have a full life and one that is blessed. Very few of us can say that we are able to lead a full life. Many people are suffering from sickness, tragedy, bad luck, oppression and struggles in life. Jesus tells us, "the thief comes to kill and destroy, but I came, so that you could have life, and in abundance". John 10:10. The question is, how did the thief (satan) enter in to our lives in the first place and take away the full life that was destined for us by God? Evil can enter our lives in different ways; through past deeds of our ancestors; through practices or objects that we encounter in our daily lives that are linked to evil unknown to us or by our own actions and intentions spoken or unspoken.

In the last number years, in my experience, I am seeing a significant increase in the number of people being affected by evil in Ireland and elsewhere. I wish to impart both a message of vigilance in these times and a message of hope, that prayer can overcome the most horrendous situations and that nothing is impossible to God.

I wish to share with you the stories of people who I have met or have contacted me with situations that they have experienced. These are real stories that have happened and they continue to escalate in intensity each year, such is the epidemic. Colleagues of mine in similar prayer ministries are having the same experience.

I am being directed very strongly now to pray for forgiveness and atonement for deeds committed in our past. Ireland has had a troubled history and under the leadership of different authorities, many atrocities have happened in the past, the effects of which still exist today.

Road accidents, deaths, sick animals or people, mysterious situations, unexplained illnesses, infestations, fears, abuse to name a few – all stem from one source.

From the beginning of 2010 I have been increasingly led to help people affected by evil spirits. People are lost and are searching for direction, but in the wrong places. New Age practices, some alternative therapies, tarot cards, Ouija boards, having ornaments of false gods and other practices have increased immensely and are to be avoided. These practices invite evil and suffering into their lives.

In the current economy, Satan is trying to get the upper hand. He is causing much pain, misery, tragedy and hardship. Many of us have forgotten about God's blessings and protection which can be obtained from prayer, the sacraments and Mass. It's time for us to stand up and take back control of our lives and this situation – everybody must play their part in God's plan. God's love and mercy is so strong and it is His greatest desire and joy to restore us to a full and abundant life. He delights in setting us free from these problems that bind us in life.

Our Lady is the key figure in the fight against the devil's tricks and is allowing these situations to be revealed, so people can be helped. She is the purest of all creatures and thus always conquers him...'the woman will crush the serpents head', Genesis 3:15.

Larry Cummins

Definitions of Deliverance and Discernment

Deliverance from Oppression, Tragedy or Sickness
The term deliverance in religious use describes the process by which a person, believed to be under the control of an evil supernatural entity called a demon or demons, is set free – delivered – from the control of that demon. In the New Testament, Jesus and some of His disciples are described as 'casting out demons' from individuals and thus 'delivering' them from the oppression of a 'demon'.

'And He (Jesus) called the twelve to Himself, and began to send them out two by two, and gave them power over unclean (evil) spirits . . . So they went out and preached that people should repent. And they cast out many demons, and anointed with oil many who were sick, and healed them.' (Mark 6:7, 12-13). At the lower end of the scale of evil, demons can be the cause of sickness or tragedies in your life. Most people wouldn't be aware that as Catholics, we have more power over demons then they have over us, **because we were baptized**. The outpouring of the spirit of God that we received at our Christening is more powerful than any evil spirit, so we have the ability to cast out minor evil attachments from our own lives, using prayers of deliverance.

Deliverance from Possession
At the higher end of the scale of evil, the Roman Catholic Church has a ritual that is used to deliver people from what is perceived as demonic possession. These rituals are usually performed by a specific religious official such as a priest, and are referred to as 'exorcisms.' There are lay people and religious from other Christian religions that have been blessed with the gift of exorcism too, however, they are few in numbers.

Spiritual Gift of Discernment
In May 2016 the CONGREGATION FOR THE DOCTRINE OF THE FAITH, at the Vatican, released the Letter "Iuvenescit Ecclesia (The Church rejuvenates)" to the Bishops of the Catholic Church Regarding the Relationship between Hierarchical and Charismatic Gifts in the Life and the Mission of the Church

'There are diversities of gifts, but the same Spirit. There are different ministries, but the same Lord. And there are diversities of activities, but it is the same God who works all in all. But the manifestation of the Spirit is given to each one for the profit of all: for to one is given the word of wisdom through the Spirit, to another **the word** of **knowledge** through the same Spirit, to another faith by the same Spirit, to another gifts of healings by the same Spirit, to another the working of miracles, to another prophecy, to another **discerning of spirits**, to another different kinds of tongues, to another the interpretation of tongues. But the one and the same Spirit works all these things, distributing to each one individually as He wills'. Corinthians 12:4-11.

The **gift of discernment of spirits and knowledge** that I received, has allowed the evil behind the problems in this book to be revealed.

Past Atrocities

Black Dog
Terri regularly visits her in-laws in north Donegal. On many occasions she saw a black dog with big red eyes, which would appear suddenly on the roadway in front of the car. However, they never seemed to hit the dog. On one occasion her brother-in-law was driving when it happened and thought he hit the dog. There were four people in the car that day and they all saw the dog. He got out of the car to discover there was no dog anywhere to be seen. Terri phoned me and we prayed for direction. It related to the flight of the earls in 1607 from Lough Swill. The O'Neills, O'Donnells and others were the reigning chieftains in the area at that time. When the earls left to go to Spain & France, the people were open to a lot of persecution. I was directed through prayer that a lot of atrocities were committed. Prayers of atonement were to be offered for these and no dog has been seen since on any subsequent visits.

French Landing
I was giving a talk in Ballina, Co. Mayo in 2004. North of Ballina, there is a Shrine to Our Lady. Nancy, who invited me, mentioned that she would always get an eerie feeling when she visited the shrine. We went there the following morning and I too experienced a negative feeling coming from the whole surrounding area. It was incredible and quite evident. We went into the prayer room there to seek direction. I was enlightened that it related back to 1798 when the French landed in Killala. Many French were taken hostage, but when they were released, they became victims of atrocities carried out on by the ruling authorities of the time. Prayers of atonement were needed for this situation. Nancy organised a novena of masses to be celebrated and also a group of people to pray the Stations of the Cross, at the shrine each day for 9 days also. When the prayers were completed, she phoned to say that the eerie feeling had ceased and that the area was now at peace and that still persists.

Munster 2010 – Heifers & Bulls getting mixed up
John phoned me with a problem he was having. He had heifers and bulls segregated on his farm. One morning when he checked on them, half the heifers were in with the bulls and the other half of the bulls were in with the heifers. He couldn't understand how it happened as all gates were secure. This happened on a number of occasions. We prayed for direction and he was being asked to pray for the atrocities committed against the Church of Ireland community (in his county) after Ireland received its independence, in the early 1920s. There was a lot of unrest and many people were murdered innocently. He didn't understand how he was singled out as his family were never involved in anything like that. I explained that the Lord had picked him out to do this task. Masses of atonement for the atrocities caused

were to be offered (one mass a month for 12 months). He was happy to take that on board when it was explained.

Problem with Drinking Trough in Tipperary

On another farm, the owner was having a problem with the water supply flowing into a drinking trough for the animals. Everything was in perfect working order, but the water would suddenly just stop flowing! After we prayed, I was directed that in the past a Church of Ireland minister lived close by and neighbours deliberately contaminated his domestic water supply. The owner subsequently got masses celebrated to atone for the crime committed. After that, he had no problem with the water flowing in to the trough.

Seriously High Number of Accidents on the N71, west of Cork City

In 2006 Kaye who lives locally became very concerned about the level of ongoing tragedies on a reasonably straight main road between Cork City and Innishannon. When we prayed about it, I was directed back to famine times. It was related to the relief schemes set up after the famine by the government and landlords of the time, to create work for so many destitute people. The scheme involved the building of walls, roads and cleaning up rivers. There was a recent documentary on RTE about this scheme. I was directed through prayer that the landlord over the scheme to build the road from Cork to Bandon agreed to pay the workers a set wage. The standard wage was approximately ten old pence a day. The landlord reneged on the amount to be paid to the workers. The workers felt extremely hurt and devastated because the wages were low enough as it was, and now they were getting even less. They cursed the road, the work they had done and the landlord. It was wrong for the workers to curse the landlord and the landlord was wrong to dishonestly reduce the wages. As a result their actions were not atoned for and the accidents started happening in 1929 many years after the road was built. I suggested that a mass be celebrated to deal with this particular situation, which she did. Kaye also arranged with a priest to drive along that part of the road while blessed salt and holy water was being sprinkled along the way. In November 2008 she phoned me to say that it was two years since they had prayed about the situation and that there were no fatal accidents since, on that part of the road.

I gave a talk in Waterfall near Cork City in October 2010 and I mentioned this particular incident. Gerry and Susan who were at the meeting were aware of all the accidents but suddenly took a bigger interest in the story and started to investigate it officially. I visited the road in February 2011. They researched the places, dates, and how many died in each accident. The earliest fatality researched was 1929. Up to 2006 where there have been approx 60 fatal accidents (from available research to date). This does not take into account all other accidents where people were severely injured. There is a particular stretch of approximately one and half miles covering the areas of Rigsdale, Annaghbeg and Toureen where the highest concentration of accidents (16 approx.) has occurred. The first known fatality was 1936 and the majority of these occurred in the last decade, one in which six people were tragically killed in the one accident. About one mile from that area in the direction of Cork city four Polish people were killed as well as five other separate accidents in that area. People from all walks of life were killed including a member of the Gardaí.

Through this research they found that the accidents extended as far as Bandon. A mass of atonement and deliverance prayers were celebrated in Innishannon. All known relatives of the victims were contacted and they took part in the ceremony. It amounted to a packed church in Innishannon. Members of the fire brigade and nurses from the local hospitals, who would have attended the accidents, were present too. There have been no further fatalities on this stretch of road since.

Accident in South West 2010
Frances contacted me about an unusual spot near a farm on a road where there were a number of accidents over the years. She told her own story about driving the car past the farm one day and suddenly 'something' took control of the car, which went over a nearby ditch and ended up in a field. She was aware that there were previous accidents more or less around the same spot. All accidents happened on the same side of the road. I prayed with her and found there was an evil situation involved. On the property where the car went out, there was a family dispute many years previous. A younger member of the family poisoned a senior member maliciously and deliberately over a dispute with property. The killer was still not at peace. Prayers and masses of atonement for the deed committed were arranged.

2009 Donegal, Road Accidents
On the main Sligo to Donegal coast road there were a number of accidents over the years. On this stretch, where there is a dip in the road, a school girl was killed waiting for the bus to pick her up. Someone driving southward fell asleep and the car swerved across the road and killed her. Her friend who was sitting beside her was uninjured. Some years previous, an aunt of hers was killed about 100 yards from the same spot. She was also waiting for a lift at the time. Many years ago, prior to that again, in the same spot, a man was killed with a horse and cart. There were other accidents there too and all happened within a span of 100 yards from each other. I was approached by a retired local lady who questioned me as to why so many accidents happened in such a small area. I asked her to get a map of the stretch of road, which she did. She highlighted all the things that happened in the general area and off shore down through the years. Around 1920, 5 RUC officers were travelling by bicycle on this very same stretch of road. They were ambushed and all were killed. I was directed that atonement needed to be made

for the atrocity caused. Two ships belonging to the Spanish Armada ran aground in 1500s opposite this area on the coast. The Spanish sailors on one of the ships were attacked by the locals with a view to robbery and some of them were killed (and they had come to help the Irish!). There were other atrocities in that area too where atonement needed to be made, including the Lord Mount Batton incident in 1979. They came regularly to Mullaghmore on their holidays. Four people were killed, including two eleven-year-olds. She arranged two novenas of masses in atonement for the atrocities that happened in her area. She had extra masses celebrated subsequently.

Being affected by an Arm

One time, coming home from Medjugorje, we got into the transfer bus at the airport in Dubrovnik to go to the plane. I got very physically affected by a man standing up in the front. He was holding the roof strap and the problem was coming from that arm. I went up and asked to speak to him. I gave him my details and he phoned me the following week as I knew we wouldn't have enough time to talk. I asked him if he had hit anyone in the past or did anything with his arm or hand, maybe write blasphemies or a mischievous letter. He admitted that he did hit somebody, but he was on good terms with that person. However, I felt he wasn't telling me the full story. Later, I got direction that he hit somebody else in a pub in England and they died as a result. He hadn't repented or atoned for his actions. Unknown to me, a year later, another family member, met this man by accident and was greatly affected by him too. I arranged for masses of atonement to be celebrated for the situation.

Ireland has led a troubled history and every town or village will have ancestral sins of the past that haven't been atoned for. It is very important to remember that the sins of previous generations can be visited upon the present generation, as well as our sins today being visited on future generations, if not confessed before we die. This is one of the many reasons why souls are held in purgatory. In December 1999, the International Theological Commission at the Vatican produced "**Memory And Reconciliation: The Church And The Faults Of The Past**" which highlights a need to pray for past generations as had been the practice for our spiritual ancestors, the Jews. "The most frequent are the confessions that mention the faults of the forebears, linking them expressly to the problems of the present generation. (34)"[3]. This document is the theological foundation for the Family Tree Healing Masses or prayers. The cure for a generational curse has always been repentance. When the Jews turned from idols to serve the living God, the curses were broken and God saved them (Judges 3:9, 15; 1 Samuel 12:10-11). Israel's sin was visited upon them until the third and fourth generations, but in the very next verse God shows his "love to a thousand [generations] of those" who love him and keep his commandments" (Exodus 20:6). God teaches us that when we sin and it is not confessed or atoned for, we can lose His blessing until the third or fourth generation that follows. He also teaches us, that when we keep his commandments, we remain under his blessing and His love and mercy lasts for 1000 generations after.

If we think something in our area needs prayer?

- First seek discernment to see if there is something that needs to be cleared.
- Seek a priest or lay person in the deliverance ministry to deal with the specific situation and use the Healing of Ancestry – A Prayer of Deliverance and Apology to God Our Father prayer at the back of the book, amending it to suit your community.
- Maybe arrange for a Novena of Masses to be celebrated.
- **Seek discernment again to confirm that the situation is at peace or if it needs further prayer.**

Curses/Piseogary

Grandfather was cursed by Neighbour

Georgina contacted me in March 2016 as her 10-year-old Son Philip was suffering from a problem with his eyes. He would say to his mother that there was something inside in his eyes, yet when she checked there was nothing apparent. When I prayed about it, it was revealed that his grandfather had been cursed by a neighbour. His son had a similar issue with his eyes too and now his grandchild was being affected in the third generation. The effect of the curse was lasting through the generations. John Gillespie encounters many incidents like this too, where unresolved issues from ancestors were not resolved or atoned for and cause sickness. To this day, curses or un-forgiveness, can result in sickness in this generation, especially cancer.

Male members of family cursed – October 2010

Testimony from Philip Carroll:

My sister Nadine left a phone message one evening to say her husband Terry was attacked by a dog and was in hospital. When I rang her back, the phone was engaged. I phoned my other sister Carrie to find out how things were, to be told that my brother John had been taken to hospital also, with a suspected heart attack. While we were talking, she said her son Sean had been suffering severe headaches that week and her husband had a near miss at work with a large metal beam that would have killed or seriously injured him. I rang John's daughter, Deborah, to see how he was. While we were speaking she said she didn't contact my mother (her granny) because she was on her own. My brother Cathal lives with her and it turned out that he too was in hospital with severe abdominal pains. The same week another brother-in-law was involved in car accident and I had been suffering from a toothache, which I rarely get. I rang Larry and he prayed over the phone with me. He said there is something sinister going on alright, but needed to pray a bit more to get direction. I was asked to say a rosary and call him the following day. When I rang him back, he said that a curse had been put on my father over 30 year go in 1979. The effects of the curse was now surfacing and affecting the male members of the family. He told us to contact a particular priest who prayed over the phone to lift the curse. After that, everything returned to normal, the swelling reduced in my jaw, John was taken out of intensive care, Cathal was sent home and Terry recovered well from his injuries. Philip Carroll, Co Louth

Farm with a number of problems to be cleared – 2010 Offaly

Alison phoned me to say the family were having difficulty with the dry stock on the farm. The animals became frightened anytime someone came to herd them. It became almost impossible to move them out of the field. They would go in different directions and would go everywhere except through the gate. This was ongoing.

They eventually rented out the land to other people, and the new tenants had the same problem with their animals. After we prayed, I was directed that in the early 1900s a work man was killed over a dispute with the owner of the farm of the time. A mass of atonement was arranged for that situation however the problem still remained the same. We prayed again and another situation arose. It was linked to tenants being evicted in the 1800s. The tenant cursed the landlord of the time and the land. I was shown small fields, the holdings of the tenants of the time. Mary confirmed that there used to be small fields there but after they bought the farm a few years ago, they bulldozed the ditches into a larger area. A deliverance ceremony to break the curse and a mass were celebrated in the house to deal with this situation, however the situation still continued. After further prayer, I was directed that children prematurely born to tenants around the time of the famine who lived on the land were not baptised. There were nine in total that needed baptism and this was also carried out.

Horses with acute respiratory problems – 2006 Fermanagh
In 2006 I was contacted by a young man called John with great concern about horses who were suffering from acute respiratory problems. The situation was so bad, that some of the horses couldn't walk seven or eight steps and were ready to collapse. Of the stable of horses he had, eight of them were affected and the rest seemed unaffected. The vet had visited but the treatment was ineffective. I prayed a Hail Mary to see if there was a problem situation and felt it was as a result of an evil situation. I asked if he has any problem with neighbours, or buying a horse from someone they had a problem with, or was there a disagreement with someone over the sale of horses etc and he said no. We prayed more and there was still an evil source that we hadn't picked up. I asked if there was something specific about these eight horses that were affected with this problem as the rest were fine. He mentioned that they had bought them at a sale in Co. Kilkenny. When we prayed further, it seemed the problem arose at this sale. I asked if one of the animals was rated far superior to the others and he said yes. Another customer was interested in this particular animal and came solely that day to buy it. John had outbid him fairly and he was highly annoyed. He put a curse on them as a result of not getting the animal he wanted. He didn't know who this person was. I advised him to have a deliverance ceremony carried out on the animals and suggested a particular priest to carry this out and Mass celebrated. After four days, he called back to say the horses were getting better and they were over the moon with delight.

Female Line of Family Cursed
I have a friend called Billy Jones in the north of Ireland, who also has the gift of discernment and is guided to help those in bondage too, i.e., people who have been subjected to the force, power, or influence of evil. Here are two of his stories relating to curses and there are others later in the book.

I work closely with Larry on many issues and all sorts of problems seem to come to me. A family in our area was affected by a lot of tragedy. It seemed to be affecting the female line to a greater degree. I discovered that there was a curse put on this family in the past. It transpired that a neighbouring woman was to marry one of the sons in this family but his mother didn't like her and put a stop to it. After speaking with Larry, we discovered that this woman cursed the family, especially any woman who married into it. This curse also seemed to affect the women in later generations in the family. We both prayed the Pray of Protection for Freedom from Curses & Evil over the phone a number of times to deal with the curse. We had masses of atonement said for the neighbour who placed the curse as she is now deceased. All seems to be fine with the family now. In another case, a local farmer purchased a farm from a neighbour. It was the talk of the locality at the time. No one could figure out why the farm was sold in such a hurry and probably cheaply. Over the years the animals on the farm would often take sick and wouldn't thrive. The farm passed on after the farmer's death to his son who continued to keep animals there. These animals also suffered from various illnesses and ill thrift. It became clear to me that something was wrong and I discovered that the original owner was cursed by a neighbour after a dispute and he sold the farm because he couldn't take any more losses. A priest was contacted and performed a ceremony on the farm and masses of atonement were offered for the neighbour. All seems to be well now. Billy Jones, Northern Ireland

Affected by her local seaside

Teresa from Co Kerry is now in her 70s and came to me in London with her husband in November 2010. She was born near Dingle Bay, by the sea, but for all her young life, she found it very stressful to go the sea or stay there for any length of time. If she went to the seaside, she would get very physically affected and would find it almost impossible to breathe and would have to leave. In later years she moved to England and when she went to the seaside over there, it had no effect on her or on other seasides in Ireland if she came home to visit. We prayed about that and I felt it was coming from an evil source. Going back a couple of generations on her granny's side of the family, there was a dispute over a boat and lobster fishing with a neighbour. Whatever happened in this dispute, her Granny's family got cursed. There was a lot of tragedy in her family subsequently. Her dad was killed with a horse & cart when she was quite young. Her uncle was drowned while fishing at the age of 15. Her brother died in an accident in America. Another brother died tragically too at home. I asked her to have a deliverance ceremony carried out to lift the curse put on her family. I also asked her to forgive the neighbours who put the curse on her family, and to pray for them as some of them were still not at peace. She was happy to carry this out. She is the only one of her family to survive the curses.

Problem with Lame Bulls, Tipperary

Jeremy called me in 2010. Over the previous few months, he had gone through a series of stock bulls. He would only have them a few days or weeks and they would get lame. Each time he bought a replacement bull or got the loan of another and again they all got lame. In total, he had the services of five bulls. After we prayed, I was directed to a situation that went back to his family in 1935 when the family were breeding pedigree bulls at the time. Some bulls broke out into a neighbour's field and caused a lot of hardship. The neighbour was very annoyed over the disturbance and cursed the animals. Jeremy went to a priest in the deliverance ministry and got the curse lifted. I was speaking to him again in Feb 2011 and there has been no problem with subsequent bulls.

Ten Day Old Calves dying in South Tipperary

Josephine called me in February 2011. For the last 10 years they had consistently lost about 25% of their calves. All would have died when they were about 10 days old. As farmers, they were very conscientious and looked after their animals very well; however the calves would suddenly get sick and die without a cause. The vet had no answer for the problem. Up to February 2011 they had already lost two calves out of 10 cows. Some of their animals were beef cross and they normally sold these calves. After we prayed, I was directed that, 10 years previously, unknown to them, one calf they had sold to somebody, died not long after the owner bought it. The calf they sold was only 10 days old and the new owner cursed them as a result of his misfortune, but no fault of theirs. Hence, the link to the calves dying at ten days old. Josephine made contact with a priest straight away and there have been no further deaths.

Cursed by Squatters

Testimony from Eileen Cahill

Over 32 years ago my husband Tony got very sick, vomiting continuously, unable to keep anything down. This sickness came on him suddenly, feeling fine one moment to looking ashen and feeling unwell the next. It was like a dark cloud enveloped him and there was no way out. I would take him to the doctor and he would get so dehydrated he had to be hospitalised, put on a drip, given medication to stop the sickness. Eventually he'd make a recovery after a few days. In the early days, many investigations were carried out, nothing undue was found, hence no diagnosis. On many occasions, this whole scenario would commence again as soon as he came home from hospital and could last for weeks or months on end. He lost a lot of weight during this time from being a big strong healthy man to up to four stone lighter. Private treatment was sought during those bouts of sickness but no diagnosis was made. Every time my doctor saw me coming he would say 'not again'. This continued from year to year and all we could do was pray and trust in God's mercy. The last time it happened (two years ago), Tony received the Sacrament of the Sick. We made contact with Larry and had many people praying Rosary Novenas, Divine Mercy Devotions etc. Prayer support was so powerful when all else fails. Larry phoned back and shared a direction that he received regarding an incident that happened in early 1980. Tony confirmed that this was correct. His friend Pat had bought a house in London in 1980. On the day he received the key from the Estate Agent, he found that a group of squatters had already moved in. He was bitterly disappointed and didn't know what to do. He got a number of friends, including Tony, together to help him evict the squatters. They were successful and had a peaceful eviction; however, one of the girls cursed them. Naturally Pat and his friends never realised this. As a result, Tony suffered the consequences of the curse all those years.

We then contacted a priest in the deliverance ministry. Holy Mass was offered for all the people involved including the girl who cursed them. Tony had to forgive her for her wrong doing. The curse was lifted and to this day, thank and praise God, no further sickness has occurred. – Eileen Cahill, London

Accident Prone

Molly visited me in late June 2011. She is in her 30's and as long as she can remember, she has been accident prone. She has been hospitalised quite a few times, but was never in a really serious accident. The previous week, a colleague at work noticed a problem with her eye and suggested she see a doctor. She cycled to a nearby hospital to get it checked out. On the way back, she was hit by a car and knocked off the bicycle. She was taken by ambulance from the scene back to hospital again! She suffered bruising but nothing was broken. Another one of the several trips to hospital. Through prayer, I was enlightened that she was conceived out of wedlock. Her uncles were very annoyed on hearing that their sister was pregnant and cursed the baby. The baby (Molly) was subsequently adopted. Since her visit, she has arranged to meet a priest to have the curse cleared.

West of Ireland – Loss of Cattle

In Jan 2011 John Clare, called me. He had lost 24 cattle of different ages in the previous 12 months. He had a problem with a neighbour whose animals were trespassing on his land. When the neighbour was asked to sort it out, he wasn't very co-operative. When John suggested he would fence off the area himself again, there was no co-operation and became aggressive. After we prayed the problem lay with the neighbour who had cursed John. I advised him to see a particular priest to lift the curse and have a mass celebrated also.

Piseogary (Witchcraft, Irish Style)

In days gone by, it would have been common practice to put eggs in hay or potato drills, hang a dead cat off a gate, meat on land, silage or other areas of the farm or farmhouse, to cause ill will towards someone. This practice seems to hold the person in bondage in an evil way. Sadly, this practice still exists today in certain parts of Ireland and it's a very serious matter.

Letter from Thomas Sheehan, Munster, 2010

Dear Larry

My father died in 1970. I was young and able and not afraid to work. I had a suckler herd of 56 cows, 100 breeding sheep, 20 sows and 20 young sows for breeding purposes. One night a friend of mine called to the house and towards midnight we went to the yard to check the pigs. I had 18 pigs, but when we counted them, there were 19. There we found an extra diseased pig that wasn't mine. How it got there I don't know. My friend turned white and said 'that will break you'. I had strong faith, so I put holy water on the pig, injected it with whatever I had available at the time. I cured the pig but I couldn't rear my own pigs after that. My vet said to me I can't cure your pigs and that somebody has put a curse on them. I had to sell every pig, I had in the yard. After that my cows started to go wrong. They aborted and a lot of them died. Out of 56 cows, I was left with 5 and my sheep produced only a half crop of lambs. My mother had 20 hens going well. She said to me to have faith as the hens were laying so well, that they were buying the week's messages and we will be OK. That night the fox called and took 16 hens. At that stage my total stock in the farm was five cows, four hens, 100 sheep, one dog. I had no money, so I got £12,000 from the bank to get started again. I changed from a suckler herd to a milking herd. I bought in good quality in-calf heifers but some of the best ones died. Of the ones that went well, 38 of their calves died that year. I got a mass said in the house and got the farmyard and the land blessed. The deaths continued on. One day, a neighbour called and asked how things were going now? I said 'things are looking better'. There are three heifers in the field and they will be cows next year and I will be coming on bit by bit. As we were talking, one heifer dropped dead. In 1973 I got engaged to Maria. I remember saying to her 'the situation in my farm was very bad and it wasn't a place to bring a young girl into'. She said 'I have my teaching job. We will be OK'. We got married in July 1974, but while we were on our honeymoon, one cow and two weanlings died. That was the last of the deaths on the farm. We were married 2☐ years when one morning my wife had a bad car crash as she was going to work. She was knocked out at the accident; her head hit the passenger door. Her health gave up after that and it was continuous hospital and doctors visits for the remainder of her life, which was 33 ☐ years. She died in July of this year (2010). My daughter Lauren at the age of 13 was struck down with a very rare illness. She has it now 22 years. There is no cure and is very sick at times. We are praying for miracle. You mentioned to me to get salt blessed and sprinkle it around the farm. I hope to do it shortly. If you can be of any help, I would appreciate it very much. I will phone you in a few days. Yours, Thomas Sheehan

Thomas later informed me that meat was also found on his land. After we prayed, I was enlightened that a neighbour was very jealous of him. This man is now deceased. We had a novena of 9 Masses arranged to atone for the jealously and ill will that was caused by the neighbour. There was a subsequent deliverance ceremony and mass carried out in February 2011. There have been no further problems on the farm since and the neighbour is now at peace in heaven.

*It was good for Thomas to have the mass celebrated originally and have the farm blessed etc, but the damage was already done at this stage, so it needed **specific prayers of deliverance (the correct words) to be said to undo the damage caused.***

Grandmother Caused Bad Luck on the Family

Testimony from Margaret

I work in an office and became aware that the office machines and software on our computers started acting up. This continued for a number of weeks and every time it got fixed it would break again. It became very frustrating. I contacted Larry and after prayer, it turned out that one of the managers, Jenny, had been cursed indirectly by her grandmother on her father's side. Larry said that the grandmother was a lady who used to get up to a lot of devilment and piseogary. This could involve placing raw meat in someone's field or they could place eggs in hay to wish bad luck on a neighbour. These actions have their foundations in witchcraft. As a result of her grandmother's activities, bad luck fell on the family. Her brother died of cancer as a young man and Jenny herself has several accidents down through the years, none of which she caused. She was badly injured in one accident and spent time off work in rehabilitation. She had ongoing back problems and was unlucky in love. I didn't say anything to Jenny about what I found out as she wouldn't be open to praying or have a faith. We had a deliverance ceremony carried out for her and the family. Since then, her back problems have reduced so dramatically that she is medication free. She has since met a lovely man, and is now married.

Margaret Behan, Waterford

Sick Animals

Joe and his son-in-law always bred high class dairy animals. Quite a few animals seemed to be afflicted with a twisted gut/stomach which blocks their digestive system. He would have to roll the animals back and forward to rectify the problem, but it didn't always work and within 48 hrs they would die. This was happening on an on-going basis since 2005. It was getting worse and he was terrified. One day he found raw meat hidden in the silage that the cows were eating. He was very alarmed over the discovery as it was an evil deed often associated with piseogary. After we prayed, I was enlightened that someone in the locality was responsible for this and was known for it. He arranged for a priest in the deliverance ministry to block the evil coming from this situation. The cows have been fine since!

We do not realise the effect a curse can have if said impulsively. Curses can remain dormant for many years and can then suddenly surface at a later point in time. This can often be in the next generation or it might even skip a generation. We have to be mindful of what we say – words are very powerful. You can see from the stories above how wishing bad luck on someone *can work* and the severe effect it can have.

Likewise, the words of prayers are equally powerful and again you can see how these situations have been cleared through specific deliverance prayers.

If I know that I or my family have been cursed, what should I do?
- First seek discernment to see if there is something that needs to be cleared.
- Seek a priest or lay person in the deliverance ministry to deal with the specific situation and use the Prayer of Protection for Freedom from Curses & Evil at the back of the book.
- **Seek discernment again to confirm that the situation is rectified or if it needs further prayer.**

If I have cursed someone or used piseogary...what should I do?
- Go to confessions and ask for forgiveness. You won't be condemned and no sin is too great to be forgiven.
- Have a deliverance mass celebrated in atonement for those you have cursed or wronged.
- Say the Prayer of Forgiveness at the back of the book.

Jealously

There is *legitimate* jealously which is based on love which we'll cover a little later but there is also *illegitimate* jealously based on envy. This is a common struggle and envy leads to fighting, quarrelling, and every evil thing (James 3:16, 4:1-2).

Bad Milk

Marian contacted me from their farm in the west of Ireland in February 2016. The milk that they were supplying to the local creamery was getting a poor rating when it was quality tested. When the creamery lorry came to collect the milk the reading of the tank temperature was different to the test reading. The test reading was a lot higher, yet when they calibrated the tank, it was working okay. Over a number of weeks each submission was getting an unusually high reading of contamination, which they found very strange. It was tested and retested and even the creamery manager was very surprised as they had been supplying the creamery for years without any issue before. After we prayed about the root cause of the problem, it was revealed that a neighbour was resentful towards them and was deliberately casting spells on their cows which resulted in contaminated milk.

Since February 2016, I have been in contact with approx 8 farmers who were cursed by the very same neighbour. All farmers experienced tragedies and deaths. One farmer lost three cows; two broke their hips, which is highly unusual. The other animal was in calf but wasn't due to calf and excreted not only her womb but also her stomach. The vet had never come across anything like this in his experience before and naturally the animal died. On another farm, a cow died each day over three consecutive days. The vet couldn't find any cause of death. I arranged for each of them to have deliverance ceremonies carried out with a priest and to block the effects coming from their jealous neighbor and to also pray for him. They even included protection for all farmers in the whole county and the effects are now blocked. This is one of the most serious cases of farm jealously that I have come across.

Milking Shed

In a neighbouring county, a farmer was having a problem with the automatic feeders in his milking shed. One of them was continually going out of order and the service engineer couldn't find the problem. When we prayed about the root cause, it was revealed that someone in the locality was jealous of his farm. He was a neighbor who called regularly to the house. We did the prayers of protection from freedom from curses and evil from the back of the book and once the prayers were said, the service engineer was able to fix the feeder. The feeder is back in working order again now.

Family Division

I met Robert in Medjugorje in 2016. He was in his late 60's and had a troubled life. There was never peace between his brothers and sisters and there was much division in the family. He married and had four children but his son committed suicide in his early 20's. His wife never recovered from the tragedy and became suicidal herself. She subsequently was diagnosed with cancer and died. There was further division within his own children after she died and some of them stopped talking to him. He also noticed that the kitchen in his house was particularly colder than the other rooms in his house. When I prayed about the situation, I was firstly directed through prayer that back in the 1940's his grandfather was given a house by the land commission. This resulted in jealously from a neighbour who cursed the family. This curse had caused division among the subsequent generations of his father's family. When we prayed about the kitchen, it was revealed that the house was built on a sacrifice site which dated back to 1475. We prayed the prayer of protection from Freedom from Curses and Evil in the back of the book and changed the wording to suit Roberts situation. On his return to Ireland, Robert immediately arranged for a Mass of deliverance to be celebrated for his house. The priest said it was one of the worst cases he had encountered. He contacted me a week after the ceremony to say he had met his family at an anniversary mass and there was a dramatic change in their manner and even their looks! Their faces had a positive expression. He even noticed that he felt so much better in himself and many people commented on how well he looked too as they could see a dramatic difference in him.

Rats in Donegal

George returned to Donegal after spending a number of years in England. He bought a site from Andy and built a house. A number of years later he decided to build an extension on to his house and also built a second house on the same plot of land. He built the walls of the extension but then left it for over a year before finishing it. He finished the extension, but when they went to live in it, suddenly rats and mice appeared. He trapped approx 16 rats in the house. The mice would go up along the legs of the bed and soil the bedclothes. First he thought the mice and rats came out of the walls. This wasn't the case. These were evil spirits in the form of mice. Andy came to George asking him to buy extra land beside him which he did, however there was another neighbour who unknown to him was also interested in this plot of land and became jealous after George acquired it. They arranged a deliverance ceremony and prayed the Prayers of Protection for Freedom from Curses & Evil regularly. George's wife phoned me in 2010 with delight to say all the mice and rats were gone.

Problem Wedding Dress

Patricia contacted me in March 2016 as her daughter Sheila was in Australia and was coming home to get married. She was getting her wedding dress made in Australia. The dressmaker was doing well until she got stuck finishing off the bodice. Sheila gave the dress to a second dressmaker and she was having problems finishing the bodice too. A third person also had difficulty. When I prayed it was revealed that some of her friends was jealous of her getting married. We did the prayers of protection from the back of this book and when she gave the dress to the fourth dressmaker, the obstacle was removed and there was no problem getting it finished. Despite all the problems beforehand the mother of the bride said it turned out to be the best wedding she was ever at.

Joe Jackson – Dec 2010

Joe called me after his grandchildren visited one day. The children were sitting around the table and suddenly it rose off the floor and fell with a bang as if someone lifted the table and then let it go. Naturally, they were very frightened. After we prayed for direction, I was enlightened that a lady who lived a few miles away was jealous of him. He would be known locally as a pious and good man and this lady was envious of the good works that he did. He phoned a priest in the deliverance ministry who prayed with him to block the jealously coming from this lady. Since then there has been no further disturbances.

Ulster - Lost 50 Cattle

Eddie Pilkington called me in 2009. He's a farmer and in the previous two years, he had lost over 50 animals. He would go outside and find dead animals with no reason for their deaths or no explanation. There would have been no indication of sickness. Eddie and his family lived on the home farm. There were also problems in his marriage. His wife stated that she felt an eerie felling around the place, from the first time that she went to live in his family home. Then mice appeared in the house. They put down a lot of traps but never seemed to get rid of them, no matter how many they caught. Every time a mouse got caught in a trap, it had a terrible physical effect on his wife and eventually she couldn't cope with the situation any longer. She decided that the family would move from the house. They left the house but his marriage came under great strain because of everything that was happening.

We prayed for 1☐ hrs, trying to see where the problem came from. I sensed a jealously situation and felt that he was cursed also. He would have had contact with a lot of people in the cattle business. After a lot of prayer and sorting out, the problem lay with his late uncle. Eddie is very talented with looking after animals and his uncle was very jealous of his ability. His uncle cursed him and had a lot of ill will against him. I was directed that his uncle hated the ground he walk on. I suggested a deliverance ceremony and mass to be celebrated in the house where this took place. I advised him to go to a certain priest to lift the curse and any other evil effects that had been put on Eddie. He phoned me when it was complete and he felt an immediate transformation in his family, especially his wife. There were no more mice to be seen either. I feel the mice weren't real, but evil spirits in the form of mice.

He phoned me again in January 2011 to say that there was no major loss of animals since the ceremony was performed. He says he takes my book 'Please! Pray for Us...We Need Your Help – *The Holy Souls in Purgatory*' everywhere he goes and says a prayer of protection in the back of the book regularly. He was like a different man and said that there has been a dramatic change in everything, even his marriage, since then.

South West – Sick Show Animal
I was contacted in 2009 by Bridie. Her family exhibited cattle in fat stock shows, normally held in cattle marts. They were very successful and often won top prizes. She became very concerned about things that were happening to the animals as they were getting ready for the shows. A particular animal got very sick and was losing weight rapidly. The vet was brought out but he couldn't ascertain what was wrong as it didn't respond to any treatment. When I prayed with her, the problem resulted from one of their competitors in the fat stock shows, that were jealous as a result of their success. I asked her to contact a certain priest to pray with the animal. That was carried out two days later and the animal recovered straight away. The priest also blocked the jealously, which caused the problem in the first place and everything has been fine since.

2009 – Horses going to Holland for show jumping
I was contacted by Joan. Her son and others were going to a show jumping event in Holland. Shortly before the event, the horse reared up but then fell on his rump and got injured. The horse was taken for veterinary treatment to deal with the problem and was given a clean bill of health. They went to Holland with the animals, but when they got there, the horse got lame and they couldn't compete. He was Ok leaving Ireland but when he came back the vet discovered a blood clot. I was directed that her son was a very good rider. Joan was able to confirm this. Somebody in their party was jealous. I advised her to go to a particular priest to have the jealously blocked.

2010 – Heart Palpitations
Testimony from Michaela Jennings
In January 2010, I started getting heart palpitations, late at night and when I was resting. This continued for a number of months, I lost all energy, found it difficult to sleep and became very fearful and insecure in myself. All medical tests proved

inconclusive. I eventually contacted Larry and when he prayed, he was told that a good friend of mine was secretly jealous of me. I was shocked and felt sorry for them as I couldn't see what they had to be jealous of! I arranged to attend a Mass of the Precious Blood, for protection from any envious thoughts coming from my friend and was asked to say a prayer of protection before I met them again. My health has returned to normal since. Michaela Jennings, Carlow

Talented Family from Zimbabwe
I met Louisa in London in Nov 2010. There were seven sisters in the family and none of them were married or in a steady relationship. She had a fantastic personality and was very good looking. She mentioned that all her family were very good looking and very talented. Through prayer, it was revealed that back in Zimbabwe, they had a neighbour that was very jealous of her family because of their ability and good looks. When I explained the direction I got, it made sense to her. I suggested that she arrange a deliverance ceremony to block the jealously coming from the neighbour.

Accidents outside Dentist Surgery
My sister contacted me in November 2010. On a visit to her dentist in London she noticed that the wall adjacent to the surgery was knocked, by someone who had crashed into it. The receptionist said that this happened on a continuous basis and there's no explanation for it. She made a comment that there must be some sort of spirit or something causing it as there had been so many accidents. Through prayer, I was directed that a man was murdered in 1900s with a horse drawn cab. There was jealously among the cab owners of the time as he kept his outfit in pristine condition. Masses of atonement were to be celebrated for the person responsible for the crime. That was carried out and up to June 2011, there have been no accidents since.

What can we do to stop Jealously?
Starting with ourselves...
- Try not to be jealous or compare yourself to someone else, as there will always be people greater and lesser than yourself.
- The grass may not be greener on the other side. Some people seem to have it all, but behind closed doors it could be a different story.
- Be thankful for what we have. **Each one of us is so special in God's eyes** and he has a specific plan and path for each person on earth – yours is unique even though it might not be apparent.
- Material things will come and go, so try 'not covet your neighbours' goods or anything else that belongs to them'. God in his wisdom knowing how big a problem this would be, even included it as one of the 10 commandments. God knows us so well and what a major weakness it is in the human condition.

If I have been jealous of someone what should I do?

- Go to confession
- If you know you have harmed someone, arrange a Mass of Atonement to break the effect caused to others by your jealously
- Start thanking God for all the graces and blessings that you have in your life and trust that he will provide you with what you *need* in life, and not what you *want.*

The Effects of Unforgivness

Child Sick as a result of Unforgiveness from Abuse
Testimony from Billy Jones

Mary came to me with her nine-year-old daughter Orla who had been suffering from severe headaches and vomiting. She also had tingling in her fingers. She had a brain scan and lots of other medical examinations done but the results all came back clear. Her GP at one point indicated that she was faking the symptoms but this was clearly not the case. Quite soon after I put the crucifix on Orla, I realised her sickness was coming from a spiritual form. After some more prayer I was able to discover that her grandfather was not at peace. He had a poor relationship with his son, Orla's father, mentally torturing him on a daily basis. To sort out this situation a lot of prayer was to be said for him in the form of masses and he needed to be forgiven by his son. After a lot of discussion the son said he would forgive him. Orla's symptoms disappeared but after two weeks came back as bad as ever. After more reflection and praying with Larry over the phone I discovered that the son hadn't done as he said and forgiven his father. When he realised his mistake he immediately forgave his father and had all the masses said for him. From this point the situation changed. Orla's sickness disappeared and she has been well now. For the past eight months she hasn't missed a day at school since. The home situation is also better as the child's sickness was causing conflict between her parents. Billy Jones, Northern Ireland

Abusive Father and Unforgiveness
Two brothers Paddy and James (one a Garda sergeant) made contact with me about their abusive father, who beat them all when they were young. It has affected everyone of the family all their lives. They hated the sight of him and he didn't treat his wife nicely either. James was particularly bitter towards his father. I asked him to try to forgive and arrange a mass for atonement for the way they were treated. Naturally he found it difficult to accept what I had said considering all the hurt that had been caused. I explained that if he got married the feeling of bitterness would continue into the next generation and would be likely to affect his own marriage. We prayed seven Our Fathers, Hail Marys & Glory Bes. After reciting the prayer, he said he felt a new person and I could see that his face had changed to a peaceful appearance.

32 years of Oppression
I was approached by Agata from Eastern Europe when in Medjugorje in 2016. She had moved to the UK, and regularly experienced paranormal activity in her home and her life was in constant turmoil. She was mentally tormented. Her father was a nasty man and cursed Agata and her sisters from the time they were born as he had always wanted boys. His alcoholism caused

untold hurt in the family and there was a lot of anger, tension, bitterness and resentment. She confirmed that her grandfather was also a nasty man and treated her father terribly too as a child. In her village, there was also a lot of witchcraft activity. She had four exorcism ceremonies, however she still didn't feel free. She felt she was possessed by some entity. When we prayed, I was directed that she needed to forgive her father for his hatred towards his family and her grandfather too. A colleague of mine in the deliverance ministry also detected witchcraft, blood sacrifice and paedophilia coming down her mums family tree and that forgiveness was needed for this too. Agata mentioned that this made sense as she often remembered the people in her village calling her Mum and her Aunt witches. We prayed with Agata to help her find the grace to forgive her father as the prayers wouldn't take effect until this obstacle was removed. We also suggested that the priest performing the exorcism use the monstrance, as this proved very effect in previous deliverances. After she returned back to the UK, she arranged for another exorcism ceremony and specifically mentioned the issues that had to be delivered. When we prayed subsequently, I was getting that Agata had indeed found the grace to forgive her father and the last exorcism resulted in freedom from oppression after 32 years.

Family Suffering from an Abusive Father
About four years ago, Shauna came to visit me. She told me there were eight in her family. Her Father was dead, and had beaten all of them growing up. He didn't drink, but he physically abused every member of the family. We spent two hours talking, praying and discussing the family situation. During the course of the conversation I was directed that there was one family member that he beat more than the rest. Shauna confirmed that it was her sister Mary, the youngest of the family. Mary looked after him when he was dying, but he never made any apology. Shauna passed the remark, 'if he hated us so much, why did he have so many of us?' There was a great tension and fear always in the house when he was around. Anytime talk of her Dad came up in conversation between the family, she wouldn't sleep that night. That continues, even to this day. Because of what her mother went through, she couldn't see herself getting married and has stayed single. They had a mass of atonement for the hurt that he caused them and also a family tree mass. Naturally some of the family found it very difficult to forgive.

If your spouse or parent is abusive, they are lacking in love. Maybe they are coming from a place of hurt or it could be coming down through the generations. Maybe they have never experienced love and therefore can't give it. On their behalf, call down the graces and blessings from the sacrament of baptism that they received when they were christened and ask the Lord to cover them in his precious blood to bless them and fill them with his love. Picture them at the foot of the cross and on their behalf say, 'I love me, because Jesus You love me, because You died for me on Calvary'. You can use this prayer for anyone you know who is lacking in love.

To forgive someone who has hurt you so much is probably one of the hardest things anyone could be asked to do.

- **Forgiveness starts with a mental decision.** To forgive someone is simply an 'act of will' or attitude. To forgive someone is a testimony of strength and maturity, and not a sign of weakness. Maybe all you can offer today is, 'I want to forgive you, but right now I'm struggling.' Ask God to grant you the graces to carry this out.

- **Forgiveness doesn't mean you are giving in to or accepting what happened.** It doesn't excuse or negate the incident. The other person will be held accountable for their actions before God.

- **Forgiveness is not the same as reconciling.** We can forgive someone even if we never can get along with them again.

- **Forgiveness is based on our attitude not on others' actions.** There will always be people who will hurt us in life. It's how we deal with it, is what matters. Ask God to 'change me and bless them'.

- **Forgiveness is a process.** It might take some time to work through our emotional problems before we can truly forgive.

- **Forgiveness does not mean we now have to return to being the victim.** Forgiveness is not letting these actions recur again and again. We don't have to tolerate, lack of respect or any form of abuse.

- **Forgetting does not mean denying reality or ignoring repeated offences.** Some people are obnoxious, mean-spirited, apathetic, or unreliable. They never will change. We need to change the way we respond to them and quit expecting them to be different.

- **We have to forgive every time.** If we find ourselves constantly forgiving the same person for the same hurt though, we might need to take a look at what we are doing with the other person that sets us up to be continually hurt, attacked, or abused. Sometimes it is necessary to have a gentle chat with someone to ask them why they feel the need to behave this way with you and are they aware of that?

- **We still have to forgive, if they don't repent.** Even if they never ask, we need to forgive. We should memorize and repeat over and over: Forgiveness is about our attitude, not their action.

- **We don't always have to tell them we have forgiven them.** Self-righteously announcing our gracious forgiveness to someone who has not asked to be forgiven may be a manipulation to make them feel guilty. It also is a form of pride.

- **Forgiveness does not mean forgetting.** It's normal for memories to be triggered in the future. When thoughts of past hurts occur, it's what we do with them that counts. When we find ourselves focusing on a past offense, we can learn to say, 'Thank you, God, for this reminder of how important forgiveness is.'

- **At the end of our days, God will ask us how we handled the challenges He set before us.** He won't question us on the actions of others.

This is a major problem in many families. I want to go into this in detail because it is an unknown *form of evil* to carry hatred, resentment or unforgiveness towards another person. Those of you who have read my first book 'Please Pray For Us… We Need Your Help – *The Holy Souls in Purgatory* know that unforgiveness is one of the biggest reasons souls are held in purgatory. It is also one of the biggest causes of sickness and disease.

If I have to forgive someone what should I do?
- Go to confession and offer forgiveness for the person who has hurt you. Offer repentance for any hurt you have caused them in retaliation.
- Say the Prayer of Forgiveness
- Arrange a Mass of Deliverance or Healing for them as this person is likely coming from a place of hurt and include the Prayer Of Protection For Freedom From Curses & Evil and Healing of Ancestry – A Prayer of Deliverance
- Some wounds go very deep, so don't be afraid to seek counselling, if necessary

Fortune Tellers/Clairvoyants/Witches

There has been a great increase in the number of people going to fortune tellers, mediums and the like. They are advertised in the media, newspapers and it's a very lucrative business. People are paying big money to hear untruths!

Spirit in her Womb
During a visit to Medjugorje in 2014, Fr John asked me to visit Kathleen who was staying in their house and was very sick. When I prayed for her, it was revealed to me that she had been to a fortune teller on several occasions. Her family regularly went too. She had been to her local hospital in Ireland on 11 occasions. She would get awful pain in her womb area. The pain would get so severe that she was put on morphine and they still couldn't come up with a solution to her problem. We did the deliverance prayers from the back of this book and she mentioned that she experienced a heat going through her body. I was directed that she had an evil spirit in her womb and that was causing the pain. She also went to confession to Fr John to confess that she had gone to fortune tellers. I kept in contact with her over a few weeks after we returned and she remained pain free.

Janet contacted me in February 2016 as her 9-year-old girl Millie, would regularly take tantrums, swear, curse and then later would be very sorry and would tell her Mum she couldn't help it. When I prayed about the situation, the root cause of the problem was revealed to me. The mother went to a fortune teller when she was 4 months pregnant with Millie. The fetus became possessed by an evil spirit in the womb at 4 months.

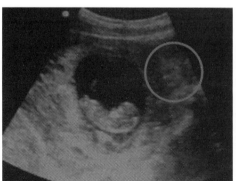 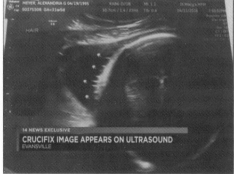

CRUCIFIX IMAGE APPEARS ON ULTRASOUND

The picture above recently broadcast in the media shows proof that this child was threatened by evil. I received further direction that this baby was under threat from abortion. Wouldn't it be better to receive a blessing for your pregnancy, like the second image above which shows a crucifix image appearing on an ultrasound, and Jesus protecting the baby.

29

Missing Toy

Testimony from Jonathan – November 2010.

I was babysitting my friend's children one day and brought them to a play centre. John aged three brought his favourite toy with him which he never let out of his sight as it was like his security blanket. Just after lunch we discovered he lost it. We searched the two rooms they were playing in and couldn't find the toy. It was big and should have been easy to spot. Naturally John was distraught. Two other adults searched the two rooms and still couldn't find it. We all searched for at least two hours but no success. The child eventually had to go home without the toy. The toy was with him all day, so we couldn't work out how it went missing. I contacted Larry to see if he could shed any light on it, as it didn't make sense. I told him the story and he prayed three Hail Marys. The direction Larry received was that the mother of the child had gone to a fortune teller or clairvoyant and as a result brought up an evil spirit. That evil spirit had taken the toy. He then prayed and commanded the evil spirit to put it back to where he had taken it from. A week later I was speaking to the mother and the toy hadn't turned up. I also rang the play centre to keep an eye out for it. A month later we went back to the same play centre and we all sat down for a something to eat. James, another child in the group walked out of the room with the toy in his hand. We asked him where did he find it and he took us in to the room and said he'd found it on top of a box there. We checked with him to see if he was playing games, but he was telling the truth. It was sitting out in the open, on top of a box for all to see. We all stared at each other in amazement as we knew how much we had searched hard for the toy. I smiled privately, but didn't say anything to the others about the evil spirit and John was reunited with his favourite toy. Jonathan Moore, Cork

Curse from Fortune Tellers

Roberta contacted me. She seemed to be having great difficulty in her marriage. There was a lot of conflict, they rarely agreed and arguments would stem from the slightest comment. It was really getting her down, as herself and her husband had naturally gotten on so well, but something changed not long after they got married. She knew there would be natural disagreements in their marriage, but there seemed to be *constant* conflict. Her husband became bad humoured, unreasonable and awkward, which was out of character from the person she knew. She too found herself becoming short tempered. This had continued for about 5 years and created great division between them. When I prayed with her, it was revealed to me that the root cause of the arguments were from visits to fortune tellers when she was younger. One fortune teller cast a hidden curse - a spirit of cantankerousness, into her future relationship to cause division. The curse remained hidden from the day of the visit until it manifested many years later after she got married. Once the curse was broken, her husband had a personality change overnight! Unaware that Roberta had been delivered, he woke up the following morning in great form, was light-hearted and reasonable. Without saying anything to him, he noticed over a few days that they had been getting on well and wanted to know what had changed. The whole atmosphere in their relationship changed once the spirit was cleared. *John Gillespie, Belfast*

Satan is root cause of many marriage break ups and many people don't realise hidden curses are planted by evil spirits when visiting fortune tellers. Angels of Light (or demons) who were cast out of heaven at the same time as Satan, roam the earth and attach themselves in hiding to people through avenues like these visits, causing problems later in life. *St Paul taught the Ephesians (6:12) that our struggle is not against flesh and blood, but against the rulers, against the authorities, against the powers of this dark world and against the spiritual forces of evil in the heavenly realms.* We have the ability to heal our own relationships by casting out any demonic influence we have encountered or on behalf of our spouse.

Possessed after visiting a Fortune Teller
Mary phoned me from England as she was concerned about one of her nephews, a twin. John was very different from his brother, James. He always seemed to be disturbed. The child was very destructive and very hard to manage. James in contrast, seemed to have a mild temperament and behaved relatively normal. Through prayer, I was told that he was with his mother when she visited a fortune teller a few years previously when he was four years old. The child had actually become possessed from being in the company of the fortune teller. I suggested that they arrange a deliverance ceremony for the child.

Disturbed Child
Imelda phoned me in September 2016. He Dad asked her to contact me as her four year old daughter Rosie seemed to be very disturbed. The tried various medical interventions but no one seemed to ascertain the problem and it continued. I asked Imelda if she had brought Rosie to any fortune tellers or any alternative practices etc, but she said no. When we prayed about the root cause if the problem, I was directed that Rosie was affected by her Mum. When we prayed further, it was revealed that Imelda herself had gone to about 6 different fortune tellers herself in the past, long before Rosie was born. Both Imelda and Rosie needed to be freed from the curse acquired from the visits to the fortune tellers. We did the prayers of protection from freedom from curses and evil from the back of this book a few times and I suggested she go to confession and to say Michael the Archangel every day to maintain her protection. We don't realise that if we pick up an evil spirit from the likes of fortune tellers etc, it can affect our children in the next generation.

People are desperate and are searching for direction. Our economy is unstable, many are lost and insecure and people have a natural curiosity about the future. Only God knows this and he wants us to trust in his plan for us...*as it unfolds* for each one of us. **It is not our place to step ahead of God.** People, who get involved in this practice, think they are being directed by angels or spirit guides which sounds safe, comforting and consoling. These directions are coming from masquerading demons who will tell you a truth from the past (to sound convincing), but can tell you some lies about the future. The devil is the master of deceit. I know of one woman who was told that she would only have another three years with her sick husband. The visit caused her a lot of unnecessary worry and anxiety over the pending lost of her husband but he eventually recovered and 15 years later is still with her.

What can we do to stop Fortune Tellers/Witches/Clairvoyants from practicing our area?
- Pray the Prayer of Protection for Freedom from Curses & Evil for them and include them in your daily prayers so that what they are involved in will be revealed to them. These people are children of God who have been caught up in bondage.
- Ask the Lord to bless them
- Sprinkle blessed holy water and salt around their premises (where possible)

If we have visited a fortune teller, what should we do?
- Go to confession, and repent for not trusting God's plan for us.
- Say the Prayer of Protection for Freedom from Curses & Evil and arrange to have a deliverance ceremony carried out, in case you and your family have carried any *unwanted guests* home with you.

New Age, Occult Practices

Excerpts from a Letter from Elaine – January 2011

My name is Elaine. I am 45 years old, married to Kenneth and have an eight-year-old son called Mark. We live in England. Nine years ago, before I was even pregnant with Mark, I suddenly started to experience strange symptoms. It would start early in the morning while I was asleep in bed. I suddenly started feeling very dizzy as if the bed was swaying. Since then, the symptoms start the same way, with a strong tension in the base of my skull and in my neck and I feel dizzy and headachy. It feels like my head has been put in to a microwave and is bombarded by radiation and being fried up. The muscles in my neck and in between my shoulder blades become very sore and so do my eyes. I cannot open my eyes in the morning, it's like I've been drugged up. I used to be overcome by intense fatigue and would drift into a sort of 'coma' for almost three hours at a time, around the time of 3pm (time I have to go and collect my son from school). If I am not neutralized by this intense fatigue, then I will be awakened early morning around 6am very suddenly by a sensation of dizziness. It always starts around 8am when I'm asleep, motionless, restful, and it catches me off guard, so to speak. For the first four years of my symptoms, the attacks were so relentless and intense that I lost more than a stone in weight and I could feel as if all my energy was being sucked away, quite literally. During all my pregnancy the symptoms did not stop and it is a miracle to me that my son Mark was born healthy. He is the most beautiful gift God has given me. Praise God! Alas, for the first three years after he was born, I was so weak that I was lying on a bed, like a vegetable in a lot of pain, especially my top half of my body. My son has never known me like I used to be, before the symptoms started. He has never seen me 'normal'. I used to be very sociable, bubbly, and enthusiastic. I have never really been a normal mum for him, cooking and playing with him. I started a series of medical investigations (in England & Europe) after the little one was born. No doctor could find anything significant that could explain the severity of my symptoms. I could be anywhere in the world, but the ordeal would continue. In 2005, some Christian friends of mine started to pray for me as nothing medical could explain what was happening to me. I very slowly started to gain weight, however 2005 was the year I reached the bottom. I felt I was dying and I was powerless. Today, I can say that the symptoms are as strong as they were nine years ago, but I have learned to survive and not panic when it starts. It is relentless, happens every week, some weeks for 5 -10 days in a row, night and day non-stop. It is exhausting. Seven years ago, I met a Nun from my parish that has been so wonderful to me and my son. She strongly suspects 'foul play' somewhere because over the years I have noticed that I would be very unwell, particularly on religious feast days like Easter, Pentecost, on family birthdays, Valentine's Day, Mother's Day etc. In particular I would dread Ash Wednesday because I would suffer so much. Any significant days in my life are spent neutralised in bed feeling unwell. I try to fight back now and get up but it is not enjoyable, as the symptoms are very strong on those days. After nine years, I cannot believe, I am still at the mercy of these 'attacks'. I cannot have a social life anymore and above all, I cannot work. I was a qualified teacher. Now I have lost my financial independence and my husband is running the family home. Beyond the frustration and the physical pain, there is this feeling of being at the mercy of something I have no control over. My husband is not catholic and I pray that the Holy Spirit will inspire him. He does everything in our marriage. I believe this is a miracle that after the ordeal I am going through, we are still together. I know God somehow sustains us. But something is preventing my healing from happening – I hope to find out with your help. Doctors have given up now. The only positive thing coming out of this ordeal is that I am closer to God, than I was before. I go to mass twice a week, but I have noticed that I feel quite unwell on Sundays now, thus preventing me from attending. At the moment I cannot see the end of the tunnel. I hope that you will be enlightened on the 'why', 'who' and 'where' of my situation when you have the time to pray for me. I truly hope that Our Lady, I call her my 'my heavenly mother' will intercede for us, so that we have some answers to help me resume a normal life. I hope for a better life than before. Closer to Jesus! May the Holy Spirit guide us, inspire us and protect us. God Bless you! Elaine

I read Elaine's letter four times when I received it – she has been through such a horrific ordeal. When I prayed, I was directed that evil was certainly at play. I spent 1½ hrs on the phone to Elaine praying and discerning. What came up was amazing. Her mother in law, Linda, never fully accepted her into the family. In addition to that, Linda is heavily involved in satanic rituals and goes abroad regularly for sessions. Elaine was able to confirm this. Elaine's illness was the result of a malicious and evil spell that Linda *deliberately* put on her. Her whole natural life was destroyed. I prayed the deliverance prayer for a whole week for her. I arranged for a deliverance team of people whom I know in the UK, to pray for Elaine's deliverance and to block the evil coming from her mother in law. As of now, things have improved greatly. She is more mobile and she had a great day during the last Ash Wednesday (2011), so much so that she was able to do the readings at Mass. This was due to the prayers of protection said by the prayer team. This is one of the most serious situations I have come across.

Subsequent to when this story was first published, Elaine did continue to improve, but after a number of months still wasn't 100% delivered. It really puzzled me why we weren't getting a breakthrough. Through the discernment of another colleague in the deliverance ministry, it was revealed that there were objects in her house and jewelry owned by her husband that contained evil. Her husband had a ring that contained a crystal gem stone that was cursed. There were scented candles that had spells cast on them and her mother in law had secretly hidden other cursed objects in the house, so she wouldn't find them. Until, these objects were removed, from the house and her presence, she wouldn't be 100% clear to receive the full healing and blessing. Sadly, Elaine didn't have the courage to speak to her husband or mother-in-law on the matter and has failed to remain in contact. We will continue to pray for her.

Possessed by attending an Evil Prayer Ring
Kate contacted me from London. She was aware she was possessed by an evil spirit. She got involved in a prayer ring or séance, that she thought was religious and above board. There were 22 involved in this and they met regularly. I was enlightened that there were people in this ring who were not holy. About a year ago, she started getting physically affected, as if there was something inside the top half of her body. She did seek help and was prayed with by a priest in the deliverance ministry. This 'thing' then moved to her womb. All through this time she wasn't sleeping at night. She was aware that others in the group were affected too. At the end of March she was prayed with again by two priests and it now seems to have moved down further in her body. As of now, she has more peace and is sleeping, but it is not fully cleared. There is a team of people in the deliverance ministry continuing to pray for her.

Bright Student Doing Very Poorly
Bridget was speaking to me in April 2010. Her grandson Barry, aged 13 was a grade A student and had been going for extra grinds to a teacher. Just after he started his tuition, he seemed to go brain dead. He couldn't focus or study, and did very poorly in exams. He couldn't learn anything. Later when his school report came out at the end of the summer, he went from being the most intelligent in the class, to the poorest student. The teachers couldn't get over it! I prayed with Bridget and was directed that the teacher was involved in the occult which in turn was having a tremendous affect on him. Bridget arranged for him to be prayed with and he was immediately back to normal the following day!

November 2010 – Bugs & Lice in London
I was approached by Maggie who had people resident in her house. One of the residents was complaining about lice or unusual bugs in her room. When the woman went to investigate, it transpired that there was a second room with the same problem. The bugs seem to be everywhere in the second room, under the mattress, in crevices etc. Pest control services were contacted and carried out the extermination. The bugs seemed to be slightly affected but they were still there. I was in London at the time and was taken to this house. I prayed outside and I was directed that one of the residents was involved in something of an evil nature which caused all the problems. We prayed the prayer of protection a number of times and over night they all disappeared without trace and haven't returned since. Maggie gently asked the lady to leave the residence.

South African – Witchcraft

A group of people were at a day of prayer in the south of England. A mother and daughter from South Africa were part of the group. On the way back, the daughter became very agitated, was having unexplained outbursts of torment and eventually collapsed on the floor of the bus. At the top of the bus a man was reciting prayers and was called up to help with this situation. He asked everyone to pray St Michael the Archangel prayer and sprinkled holy water in the bus. After a short while the daughter returned to normal. I was contacted about this situation. They were both born in South Africa. We prayed for direction and I was told that she was possessed. I arranged to speak to her mother, a very nice lady. She confirmed what I told her and said she was well aware that her daughter was possessed for 13 years as a result of meeting someone in college. After we prayed further, I was directed that her daughter wasn't affected by the young man she met in college, but it has come down through her mother's blood line from someone who was involved in witchcraft. We went back through her family tree. Her ancestry was a mixture of various European and African origin; however the witchcraft was linked to a generation of Zulus about six or seven generations previous. It was arranged that the mother speak to a priest in Ireland in the deliverance ministry to lift the possession. After the prayers were said, there was an immediate transformation in their house.

Nov 2010 – 2 Hour Exorcism

Every November I visit London for a week of meetings. Shirley came to meet me one afternoon and told me immediately that she felt possessed by a spirit since she was seven years of age. She had been seeking help with this situation but to no avail. When we prayed, I could confirm what she was telling me. In fact, all her family were somewhat affected by evil, but she was the most affected. One of the family became a Carmelite nun, but subsequently left. She too was possessed. Her family was European, but lived in South Africa for a number of years. Shirley and her sister were born there. It seemed that the family were good Catholics, but some family members had contact with witchdoctors. We prayed to see where it stemmed from. When her mother was getting married, her grandmother was unhappy with her proposed son-in-law and arranged for a witch doctor to prevent the marriage. The marriage went ahead, however the effects of the witch doctor stayed. When they found out, the family visited a second witch doctor to clear the spell from the first man, but this didn't work. From a very young age, Shirley felt affected by some outside force. The following evening, we advised her to come to a meeting in North London with a Mass and a deliverance ceremony. I informed the priest beforehand about her. After mass we started to pray with everyone and Shirley was one of the first. We put her sitting on a chair to the right of the altar and included all her family in the ceremony. The priest bought out the Blessed Sacrament in a small monstrance and standing in front of her gently commanded various spirits to leave. There were three of us praying and suddenly she jolted up out of the chair, as if on a spring. I was given a Benedict Cross to hold and was asked to participate in the deliverance ceremony. At one point in the prayer, I felt something bump off me as it ran passed me. Eventually she slipped off the chair and rolled down on the floor and her body was continually moving. After an hour of praying with her, she stood up and fell over like a statue and hit her head on the central heating pipes. She didn't even put her hands out to protect herself and remained that way for about 15 minutes. I was concerned that she was hurt, but when she eventually got up, there wasn't a mark on her head. All of this was as a result of the effect of the demons within her. All this time, we were giving her drinks of water. We continued into a second hour of prayer and everyone in the church was either singing hymns or praying for her. She moved from the chair to the floor again and her body moving all the time. After 1hr 50 minutes she was standing up again like a statue and fell face down on the floor again and stayed that way for about six minutes. She rolled over and got up and sat down on the chair and was more relaxed at this stage. I was directed by Our Lady to pray the glorious Mysteries of the Rosary, and was told that she would be alright. We all prayed the rosary and within a couple of minutes after that, Shirley was finally at peace. Shirley was possessed by many demons. As can be seen from Shirley's story, demons are always reluctant to leave the body so will put up a big fight against any prayers of deliverance. I met her the following day and she didn't seem to remember much of what happened the night before during the deliverance because what took place was a spiritual battle and not a physical one. I suggested that she say the prayer of protection daily. I have had two letters from her since and everything is still OK. Nothing is impossible to God!

Lady who thought she was possessed.

A priest in Co Meath contacted me. He was visiting a patient in the local hospital who claimed she was possessed and got fearful of the situation. He contacted his local bishop who advised him to be very careful of how he handled this person. Through prayer, I informed him that the person in question was not possessed, but had a mental problem not a spiritual one. I tell this story as it's **so important to discern before carrying out a deliverance**, as appearances can be deceiving.

Noisy Neighbours involved in Evil Practices

Testimony from Kathleen Browne

Ann and Pat are our neighbours. They met on the internet but from the time they got married, things started to change with us. They have small children who are rarely allowed out of the house, not even into the garden. We began to hear Ann screaming and shouting at the children especially early morning or in the middle of the night or if we met them out front. Larry asked us to say a prayer of protection and this certainly helped. He was directed that they were involved in evil practices.

We also phoned a priest in the deliverance ministry who prayed with us over the phone. I found chewed fruit and discovered we then had a rat. We set one rat trap and two mice traps and the following morning, we caught the rat. Larry said it was the evil coming from next door. That evening I was walking across the kitchen floor and my two feet were taken from under me (but I didn't trip) and I fractured my wrist! We then had a mass said to block anything that was coming from next door. I say the prayer of protection every day for them. The screaming and shouting through the walls have stopped and peace now reigns. 'Praise the Lord'. Kathleen Browne, London

Tradesmen involved in Pornography
Testimony from Helen Jordan
When we moved into our house eight years ago, we had a huge amount of work done. There were a lot of people working on the house at the time, including my two brothers, Kevin and Philip. We paid one man for granite for the floor but we never saw him again. I contacted Larry and was directed that he was into pornography on the internet. The other guy doing the bathroom tiling was affected by him and his dealings; went home one evening and didn't even return for his tools or his money. My legs broke out in a severe rash and no medical treatments worked. Kevin also got affected and became very irritable and snappy with everyone. Everyone could see the sudden change in him, but he didn't think there was anything wrong with him. I was prayed with by a local Benedictine priest. My rash cleared but returned five days later. This happened three times. Then we got a prayer team in with Larry's help. He was also directed through prayer that a couple with a little girl seemed to have rented the house some years before. The little girl was neglected and left in a press under the stairs. The prayer team could hear her cry. The tools left behind by the bathroom tiler were affected too, so we had to get rid of them off the premises. I had a deliverance ceremony and mass celebrated in the house to deal with all the situations and I had the little girl baptised. I continue to pray for her mother. After the deliverance ceremony in the house, the rash cleared up for good. Today we have peace. Helen Jordan, London

Work Colleague involved in Pornography
Testimony from Jason Billings
In September 2010, not long after a new colleague (Enda) joined my work I became aware of a terrible smell in the place. I complained every day and would use air freshener, but to no avail. He was an incredibly difficult and awkward man to work with. I contacted Larry and was directed that Enda was into the highest degree of pornography on the internet. Part of our work involved children and I became very concerned for them, after I found out! I reported him to our boss, without revealing what I knew. I had prayers of protection offered for him and today he is a totally different person and we get on really well now. Jason Billings, London

Sept 2010-Plasterers in London

Serena Malone called me as she had great concerns about her health. Her face had suddenly become very swollen under her eyes. She felt there was more than a health problem involved. I asked her to pray and call me back. When she rang me back at the appointed time we started to pray and she was right. I was enlightened that her problems related to some workers they had recently hired, to complete a renovation job on their house. After listing out the different tradesmen, I was directed to two plasterers who originally came from Eastern Europe. They were part of a group that were practicing satanic rituals. Every day, her face was getting worse. I advised her to have a deliverance ceremony arranged to clear the situation and have a mass celebrated too. She booked a priest for the following day and after the ceremony her face healed up immediately.

12-Year-Old Girl Possessed From Using the Ouija Board

In April 2008 I was contacted by Carmel from Kilkenny. Carmel's 12 year-old-daughter Donna had a friend Sheila also 12, who was fascinated with using the Ouija Board and not long afterwards, Sheila started to act very odd. Sheila would loose her voice and start to draw grotesque figures. Her body would go into spasm. Once, when someone went to hold her, she seemed to have the strength of five people and tossed this person aside as if she was a doll. On another occasion, she tried to commit suicide. A deliverance ceremony (which lasted four hours) was carried out on Sheila and her family. They were completely delivered at this time and they have not been affected since. Sometime later, Carmel's family (who had been instrumental in arranging the deliverance ceremony for Sheila) became affected. They experienced a grotesque smell in the house for about two years. It was so bad she couldn't invite anyone in. They could smell it through the keyhole if they were coming back to the house. A Mass and deliverance ceremony was carried out at the beginning of May and removed 95% of the smell. A second deliverance ceremony was carried out a week later and the house is now back to normal.

Ouija Board Story in London – November 2002.

My sister took me to visit a man. When she opened the door, a force of evil was coming through so strongly that I had to back away. I told her that somebody in the house was involved in something evil, but it wasn't the man we were going to visit. As I looked in through the open door, I saw a young man, looking out through an inside door and felt the problem was connected with him. We didn't enter the house at that time, but closed the front door and walked up and down the footpath outside and prayed for protection to blessed Michael the Archangel. I felt a strong need to talk to this young man and not the man we had originally decided to visit. We went back to the door a second time and we were able to walk through. He was from the continent. My sister spoke to him and I related all the directions I was receiving.

I was guided that he was linked with a Ouija Board, which he denied initially but eventually admitted that he had used it with two friends and moved glasses etc. He was very affected physically as a result of its use. I told him that he needed to have this dealt with. I was given direction not to touch or pray with him. He couldn't understand how I was able to relate all these happenings to him, having never met him before. A Mass was also to be celebrated in the house. The man subsequently left the house of his own accord.

(A lot of young people are not aware of the evil involved in messing around with Ouija Boards and other evil practices. Games Manufacturers now sell Ouija boards in the games section of toy stores as if they were harmless family fun games to play. They are highly dangerous and should not be played.)

Don't Mock the 'Our Father'
A friend told me of someone he knew who said the Our Father backwards. After that he had no luck in life, and ended up on the streets, took an overdose and has struggled to cope all his life. It's an evil way of mocking the Our Father. I know of a group who stayed out over night in tents in the woods. They carried out various spiritual practices including saying the Our Father backwards. When they were in the tents, they experienced a raging storm outside. When they looked outside it was actually quite calm. It was evil causing the so called storm. One of the group (Steven) got a premonition of two accidents. Not long after, two of the group died in two separate car accidents. What Steven saw was exactly how they were killed.

Films/TV/Books
If you have noticed lately, more and more films being produced today have a 'darker' element to them and can contain hidden influences of evil that can affect the viewer. Even pleasant fairy tales from old are being reproduced with a more sinister twist. There is a wrath of films produced now that are not suitable for watching because of the demonic and evil that is represented in them.

Woodpecker Attracting Attention
Risha called me about an unusual situation her family was experiencing in London. Over a period of a week, most of the family were seeing a woodpecker. They would notice it on the TV Arial of the house and it would be trying to get their attention. One day her husband was walking down the road and the woodpecker moved from aerial to aerial as it travelled with him down the road. She called me as all the family were talking about it. Through prayer I was directed that the woodpecker was attracting their attention to alert them to the fact that there was evil coming through some of the children's TV programmes and films. I was directed that in their daily prayers, they were to pray to block the evil coming from the TV and films.

Effects from Horror Films

Elaine contacted me to say that her daughter had become very disturbed lately. She had watched a low level horror film in school. Afterwards, all the class seemed to be very badly affected, but she was the worst. It wasn't because they found it scary, but they became affected by something evil hidden within the film itself.

My grandniece in the south east of England was affected by a horror film show at Halloween last year. Her Mum was aware that the teacher was likely to show this film and expressed her concerns but the teacher ignored her. My grandniece became very upset after watching the film and showed huge resistance to going to school. Her parents had to walk her right into the classroom in order to help her stay. The parents did the deliverance ceremony from the back of this book and everything cleared and she has no problem going to school now.

As halloween becomes more commercial, evil is given increased exposure through the different representations of objects character and themes. Please pray prayers of protection especially around this time to block the effects on families and communities.

Animated films and Cartoons

I was contacted by a Clarissa who suddenly found herself ill, had no energy, had an empty feeling inside and felt a heavy sense of oppression and darkness. When we prayed, it was revealed to me that she had watched a TV programme that contained something that wasn't right. After she named the programmes she had been watching, I was directed to a lighthearted cartoon that she had watched with her children, that had witches and wizards in the story line. Witchcraft and wizardry involve practising evil at a high level, so even a *representation* of their practices is enough to affect someone.

The Harry Potter series of books and movies have had international success in the last few years, however I wouldn't recommend you follow them as they contain 'real' curses and practices used in witchcraft. These books are instructional manuals of witchcraft woven into the format of entertainment. The series is loved by children who show Harry as a good wizard fighting evil, which causes confusion and diminishes their understanding of the dangers of these practices. In 2008 the Vatican's official newspaper L'Osservatore Romano warned the public against these books and films. The same goes for media that contains Vampires, Zombies, Devils, Demons etc. Children will always copy their heros.

Such things bring death. Now, however, you have been freed from sin and serve God. You are bearing fruit and growing in holiness, and the result will be life everlasting (Rom 6:20-22)

Alternative, Complimentary Therapies

There has been an escalation in the amount of cases involving people becoming ill from complementary therapies and alternative practices.

Evil has the Power to Heal

There is a growing number of people offering alternative/complimentary therapies. They are offered by very good living people (including religious), with good intentions and big hearts who have a desire to help those in need. Some medications can have side affects, and these therapies are seen as a *natural* way to help heal problems. In some cases, practitioners will learn how the therapy is linked in 'medically' with science etc. In a lot of cases, there will be no basis for this.

A lot of these therapies have their origins in the occult. Naturally this information is never mentioned during their course. **Evil has the power to heal** and therefore, these therapies can appear very deceiving. Practitioners will have well known religious pictures in their rooms. These therapies are very relaxing, enjoyable and clients are very likely to have a nice experience. Practitioners will see great results and customers will be delighted, coming back for more or trying another therapy.

However, there are hidden side-effects to these therapies and Satan is the master of deceit. It's only months or years afterwards that the curses from these therapies kick into action and start causing problems, no differently than curses of old affecting later generations. Possession by demons can also occur. These are the hidden curses in our modern society. Satan has great ability and can take on many disguises. Stay clear of anything to do with any sort of healing energies, bioenergy, symbols, stones or crystals.

It's important not to condemn anyone offering complimentary therapies as unknown to them, they have been tricked into thinking they are doing some *good works* (a great deceit). They feel they are offering a good service and will definitely have seen *'results'*. Don't interfere; privately pray for those involved in these therapies that if their work is not of God, that it will be revealed to them.

It is important to discern before you book one of these therapies. Remember, there is only one true healer – Jesus Christ!

Addicted to New Age Therapies

Testimony from Joanne who used to be involved in New Age...
A very good friend of mine Deirdre, offered to do **Reiki** *on me. At the time, I was in my twenties and open to lots of 'new things'. Deirdre was a very good person, went*

to Mass, sang in the choir and went to prayer meetings regularly. Reiki sounded like a really natural way to bring healing to others and you could heal yourself – this was fantastic stuff! I signed up to the first stage of becoming a Reiki practitioner. During the session, one lady claimed to have seen a vision of Jesus (Satan in disguise) while doing Reiki. I was really impressed. I was speaking to Larry, not long after this and he immediately got a **direction from Our Lady, which said 'this is not of my spirit and you are not to practice it'** loud and clear. That was fine and I didn't practice it, however two years later, I got very ill, lethargic, depressed, lost my appetite and was hit with an unexplainable illness that left me with very little energy. Medical tests came back normal and when I went to a consultant, I was told that I had a virus. This continued for a year with no improvement. Someone suggested I try reflexology. I went to a Reflexologist and everything got cleared up in four weeks. I couldn't believe it. I was so amazed that I studied reflexology and started to practice it. I had often tried out crystal healing, energy healing, went to fortune tellers etc. I attended mind/body/spirit weekends and spiritual workshops. Ten minutes after leaving one workshop, I suddenly became very anxious and I had a car accident. Luckily I wasn't hurt. A year or two later, I became depressed again and couldn't work out why as I was a very bubbly, sociable person and was content in work. Recently, I was at a talk where someone mentioned about the effects of alternative therapies and they explained what I had been doing. I subsequently had a deliverance ceremony which included praying prayers of forgiveness to close my chakra points and third (physic) eye to clear the effects that evil had caused.
Joanne Healy, Laois

After reading the above story, in the earlier version of this book, James wrote to me. He had been practicing reiki for a number of years along with other practices, however something in the story rang true for him. He said an open prayer that if this story had truth that he would be told and he would stop. Suddenly he noticed that his chakra points started to close up and he felt a great sense of peace. He couldn't believe what had happened and realised that this was the truth and stopped practicing.

Reiki can cause huge problems for people as it opens what's called chakras, (doorways through which evil spirits enter the body). Seven energy points or Chakras are identified on the body and it is claimed that when all are in balance, you feel in full health.

Reiki being practiced in the Parish Centre
I visited a priest friend at his Parish Centre on the edge of Limerick a few years ago. When I was there, I was getting terribly affected by something in an adjoining room. I asked him what takes place there and he said it's just a meeting room. I asked if it's used for anything else and he said that twice a week it is used for Reiki sessions. Many parishes offer Reiki as a 'healing' therapy and many nuns and those in religious circles are involved too apart from lay people.

Relaxation CD that caused Pain and Anxiety

Lorraine had just come back from holidays on the continent, but couldn't get to sleep. She felt very restless, anxious and was getting affected by pains in her arms and shoulders. She found this strange as she had been for some massage sessions on the beach while on holidays and had felt very relaxed. When I prayed about the root cause, I was directed that the relaxation music played during the massage, was linked to reiki. The therapist didn't practice reiki on Lorraine, only massage (which is okay), but it was the music itself that caused the subsequent problems after she returned home. This type of relaxation music is very common and seems to be used in Hindu worship. She prayed the prayers of protection in the back of this book, to specifically block the effects of any evil she picked up from the relaxation CD and all symptoms gradually eased away.

Regular massage is safe however John Gillespie has been directed to warm us against aromatherapy massage in particular. The oils themselves are probably okay and are often almond or olive oil based. However, the origin of the scent that is subsequently added can often be from eastern sources and have been prayed over with native chants which has affected people later.

Machinery affected by Pilates and Yoga

Matt contacted me because one of the production lines in his company broke down. This wouldn't be unusual and normally the on-site maintenance technicians would sort out the problem, but they couldn't get to the cause of the break down. They eventually had to ask the supplier company to send an expert on the machinery. They flew in from abroad and they too had difficulty getting to the root cause. After we prayed, I was directed that one of the girls working on the line, was attending Pilates & Yoga and unknown to her had carried the spirit of evil with her from the class. This came with her to work and started causing havoc with the machinery. We prayed and I taught him to pray the prayers of protection in the back of the book to block any satanic influence coming from his colleague from affecting the machinery getting fixed. As soon as the deliverance prayers were said, first thing the following morning, they found the reason for the breakdown. **The spirit had cause the breakdown but also prevented them from finding the root cause.**

Yoga by definition in the dictionary is 'a Hindu spiritual and ascetic discipline, a part of which, including breath control, simple meditation, and the adoption of specific bodily postures'. Yoga, of itself is not exercise, but is used as such. These postures are the positions adopted by Hindus who worship their gods. Unknown to anyone participating in Yoga as a form of exercise, they are also worshiping Hindu gods, false idols who don't bring blessing. This is a subtle deception of Satan and participants are inviting evil into their lives even those they have no knowledge of Hindu, idols or false gods. There are different types of yoga but one of the most dangerous types is the invoking of the Kundalini energy that is said to bring spiritual awakening, access to a higher consciousness's and then enlightenment where you become your own guru and control your own destiny. Chakra balancing has the ability to allow evil spirits to enter your body however John Gillespie whom I work with, dealt with a man who was possessed by an evil spirit from invoking the Kundalini spirit. It presented in the form of a snake and it took a while to deliver the man from the spirit. Yoga is not from God and doesn't bring blessing. Why not replace yoga with aerobics?

Energy Healing Lamps and Crystals Gem Stones

Energy Healing Lamps are generally made from crystals and sold to promote good health and create positive energy. Because they derive from crystals, they are in fact generating negative energy and bring bad luck. I was directed that human intervention with the stones to make them ready for sale, creates the bad luck.

Genevieve regularly felt an oppression or heaviness that she couldn't explain. To add to her woes, she stumbled on her patio and broke her hip just before a big religious event that she was organising. I visited her to see how she was and noticed the lamp in her kitchen. A friend recommended her to get one. She threw away the lamp and went around the house throwing holy water and blessed salt.

She contacted me 4 weeks later to say she was recovering well, was in great spirits and there was a great sense of peace in the house.

Crystals gem stones have long been associated with the occult. They were used to bring power, protection or take away negative energy. We remember that fortune tellers use them to acquire knowledge, often false knowledge. Crystal stones set into jewellery are okay…it's *crystal gemstones* are the ones to watch out for.

Prevented from Praying because of Crystals

I met John after a talk I gave in the west in 2008. He came to me to seek direction. To start with, I usually pray three Hail Marys, however on this occasion; I couldn't get the words out of my mouth. This hadn't happened before and I was enlightened to ask him if he had something in his pocket as it was preventing me from praying. When I asked him, he suddenly left the room and building without saying anything. I was surprised and wasn't sure if he was coming back. Later he did come back and I was then able to pray with him, this time. I asked him again what had he in his pocket and he said 'a crystal stone' and it was now in the car. I was directed that he was not to throw it over the fence, but take it straight to the dump. About a year later, I met his sister and she told me that this incident had a dramatic positive effect on him.

Religious Gift Shop selling non-Christian items

On another occasion in March 2011, I met a lady who owned a gift shop. While I was praying with her, I was directed that there were 'two things' in her shop that she shouldn't have. She mentioned a number of items, but when she mentioned 'a Buddha statue' and 'Crystals' I was affected. Again, I was directed that she was not to put them in the bin in the shop, but take them straight to the dump, so that they would be away from people.

St John of God, Brazil

Andy called me one evening. A trip to St John of God in Brazil was being organised by a local group and they wanted to check if he was *bona fide*. He is a Spiritual Healing Psychic Surgeon in Abadiania, Brazil and is known for performing visible surgery. There have been a few documentaries shown on TV. He seems to have special healing powers and some people have claimed to be healed (and evil can heal), but this man is **not of God.** One man, who went over on a trip from Ireland, noticed a terrible smell the whole time they were there. When he came back, he could get the very same smell in his home. He was eventually prayed with by a priest in the deliverance ministry and the smell disappeared. The priest became terribly affected while he was praying with him and suggested that anyone who goes out there should be prayed with afterwards.

I don't have any personal knowledge of these therapies only that I know they are not of God's Spirit. You can't say you practice your faith and allow evil into your life, because there is only one true healer. If you entertain even one of these practices, no matter how small, you are giving Satan a foothold into your life. I know of one lady who sought pray from myself and other people in ministry to solve her spiritual problems. After many months of prayer, I couldn't understand why she still wasn't cleared. I later found out that, we had cleared her spiritual problems, but they kept returning as she continued to attend energy healers and new age practices while also seeking Gods help. She was undoing all the blessings she was receiving. **We can't ask Satan AND God to heal us**. Satan is very deceptive. He is the prince of lies. He has the ability to con even the most intelligent of people! The book of Isaiah, tells us that the 'angel of light, Lucifer', was thrown from heaven to earth, not hell as we have been led to believe. He brought with him a limited ability and power. Therefore the unseen spirit of evil is *on earth* and had the ability to influence us. Satan was able to tempt Jesus in the dessert by offering Him the Kingdoms of this world (Matthew 4:8). He wouldn't have been able to do that unless he *was* the 'prince of this world'. These complementary therapies can heal, but it will only be temporary. In addition, you will receive hidden curses that will remain silent until they activate at a time in the future, often resulting in a worse illness. I've seen this several times.

For those of you who want to do more research, the Vatican Website and other church files state that the following practices and organisations are New Age/Occult practices and are therefore banned by the Catholic Church.

Enneagram, Reiki, Yoga, Rebirth, Biofeedback, Sensory Isolation, Holotropic breathing, hypnosis, mantras, sleep deprivation and transcendental meditation, Reincarnation, Channelling, Psychics, Mediums, Ascended Masters, Nature Spirits, Higher Self, Crystals, Feng-shui, Geomancy, Gaia, Human Potential Movement, Shamanism, Paganism, Druid, Wicca, Freemasonry, Neopaganism, Spiritualism, Witchcraft. This is to just name a few.

There are many who will say that the Catholic Church is 'not with the times' and need to be open to these practices. The reason these practices are banned, is because the Catholic Church understands the hidden dangers behind these practices and are trying to protect us from unseen forces.

" My people are destroyed for lack of knowledge... since you have forgotten the law of your God" - Hosea 4:6

What can we do to stop these practices in our area
- Pray a prayer of protection for them and include them in your daily prayers so that one day, their works if not of God, will be revealed to them. These people are children of God who have been caught up in bondage of evil
- Ask the Lord to bless them
- Sprinkle blessed holy water and salt around their premises (where possible)

If I have been involved in these practices or feel possessed, what should we do?
- Seek discernment
- Say prayers of protection and arrange to have a deliverance ceremony carried out, to clear you and your family of any indirect effects
- Go to confession, to renounce and apologise for your involvement in these practices (prayer at the back of the book)
- Continue to say prayers of protection

I have noticed that the spirit of evil seems to have become more aggressive in the world and can transfer easily. People are becoming ill by simply meeting someone involved in these practices. This is also happening with objects that represents evil or contains evil which I'll cover now in the next section.

Buddha Statues / Hindu Heads / False Gods / Pagan Objects

Increasingly, as we can see, practices from other lands are creeping in to our society and are now considered a normal part of everyday life. They stem from other gods.

God with a Capital G   = Yahweh, the God of Abraham followed by Christians, Jews and Islam (Muslims)

god with a small g   = Pagan, false gods worshiped in Buddhism, Hinduism, Paganism etc.

Buddhist Coffee Shop practicing Reiki

Recently I had a call from Peter. He had become ill, disturbed in himself and not sleeping at night. Not long after his wife, Imelda broke out in a rash around her head and neck. Medication didn't alleviate the problem so she too was having no sleep. When we prayed, the root cause of the problem was revealed to me. He had been to a particular coffee shop and was affected by going there. After naming a few places, I got direction about 'Jennifer's Country Cafe'. When I asked Peter if there was anything unusual in the shop, he said there were lots of statutes and religious ornaments. Some were catholic ornaments, but most of them were statues of Buddha, Hindu gods and other objects. After further enquiries it turned out that the owners were practicing reiki over the food eaten in the shop believing that they were bringing blessing to the customers. They were Catholics who had turned to Buddhism. Their intent was completely genuine. The couple arranged for a mass of deliverance to be celebrated, however the problems only eased slightly. After a second mass of deliverance, everything settled down and returned to normal for both of them.

A few weeks later, Peter's wife Imelda phoned as her friend Joan had become ill. She was having black outs and fainting spells and had been off work for 3 months. Fainting spells had happened before and consultants were able to find a medical solution, however on this occasion, the consultants were at a loss as to why it was happening again. Joan had told Imelda that she had been to the same coffee shop. When we prayed into the root cause of Joan's issues, I was directed that she had been affected from going there too. Joan realised that it was about 3 months ago since she visited the coffee shop. She too arranged to be prayed with to be delivered and is now back at work again.

Hindu god in Health Food shop

Maria visited the local health food shop to pick up some vitamins. On the way home in the car, she started to become agitated, anxious and her heart was racing. She became very overwhelmed and pulled in to the side of the road. The feeling eventually eased but she continued to feel a great sense of darkness and oppression over the next few days that didn't ease. She contacted me for direction and through prayer it was revealed to me that she had visited a shop where she encountered an evil spirit. She named a few places she'd visited in the last few days and when she mentioned that she'd been looking at a head of a Hindu god in a health food shop she had visited, I was directed that this was the cause of her health problem. I prayed the prayers of protection from the back of this book and all feelings of darkness and oppression subsided and she was free.

Converted from Buddhism
Harry is part of a prayer team that accompanies a priest in the deliverance ministry. Peter who has a gift of discernment contacted me and felt that there was some problem connected with Harry. In the past, Harry had a wonderful conversion experience from Buddhism which included Jesus appearing to him on a number of occasions. He was also given the ability to quote scripture, yet he had never studied the bible. We prayed about it. Buddhism involves adoring a false god's although on the outside it would seem to have many worthwhile attributes. I was directed that something that originated from his original way of life was affecting him and he needed to be delivered. The priest subsequently carried out the deliverance ceremony.

Child disturbed by School
Leanne called me as her daughter Emer had great resistance to going to school after she started. She would get distraught every morning. Leanne spoke to the principle and her teacher and couldn't find any reason why she was so upset. Emer herself had no problems in school or wasn't being bullied but they put the issue down to the teacher. However this problem continued into senior infants and subsequent classes, with different teachers, so they felt more was going on. When we prayed about it, I was directed that the root cause of the upset was a Buddha statue in her school, but also, they had a picture of a Buddha in their own house too. The evil from both was disturbing her.

Buddha statues affecting our mind
Jim had become friendly with a lady lately. He was well educated, had a great interest in many things, especially religion and had completed a catholic bible study course. He discovered that his new friend was interested in Buddhism and eastern religions. She practiced yoga, eastern meditation, reiki etc. They had great discussions on the differences between the religions and he had reservations about different aspects, however he still accepted gifts of Buddha statues from her as they got to know one another but didn't enter into any of the practices or her beliefs. Not long after, Jim noticed that he wasn't sleeping well,

would wake up disturbed in his spirit and started to become mentally confused. He noticed that his mind was losing its sharpness or clarity. He wasn't able to think straight! After we prayed, it was revealed to me that he was being affected by the Buddha statues from his friend. He removed them immediately and blessed the house with holy water and blessed salt and has been fine since.

Problems with House Extension

Lorcan seemed that life was throwing him a lot of bad luck. He got a sun room added to the family home which seemed to constantly leak when it rained. The builder blamed the window supplier and vice versa. They were called in on several occasions, pictures taken etc. to see where the fault lay. Then the new stove they installed started to break down. They then started to have electrical problems and the electrician couldn't get to the root cause of the problem. There were constant obstacles and issues in the house. During this time, Lorcan had to have an operation however it took him a lot longer to recover from the procedure than would be normal. When I prayed about the situation I was directed that Lorcan had two objects in his house that were causing the bad luck; a Buddha statue and an ornament that originated in Africa, where witchcraft is still widely practiced. We need to be vigilant of the types of ornaments that come from non-Christian countries as we won't always know what they represent in a pagan practice or what prayer or chant has been invoked over them. This prayer comes home with the object and then activates in the person's home, causing problems.

Practices from Cambodia

Recently Noelle volunteered to carry out some missionary work in Cambodia. Naturally it was a challenge working in a third world country, the heat and lack of any luxuries and not always sure what animal you were eating! They serviced the poorest of the poor who had no houses or schools in the jungle areas. It was very tiring work, but very rewarding. After she came home she was unwell for a few weeks and put it down to the tough time she'd had abroad. A few months later, she had an accident and put her back out. A short time after that she hit her head accidentally which caused severe concussion and was out of work for approx. 6 months. She continued to have a lack of energy and felt heavily oppressed. People would often say that she had no luck since she came back from Cambodia! She decided to check it out and I could confirm that the root cause of her bad luck and health was a spiritual force that she came in contact with in Cambodia. She explained her findings to a priest to pray a deliverance prayer with her. As he was praying with her, she could feel a heaviness lifting from her and before he was even finished she knew she was healed and delivered. She was set free. This is the truth, and the truth (God's blessing) will set you free." John 8: 31-32.

Marianne also visited Cambodia on holidays, but shortly after coming home lost all energy. She had visited various consultants and none of them have been able to help her. Her condition became so bad that she had to give up work and became bedridden. After hearing about Noelles visit to Cambodia above we prayed about Marianne's case. It was confirmed to me, that the root cause of her illness was as a result of a spiritual force she encountered when she visited there too. Many countries in Asia, South Pacific etc practice Buddhism, Hinduism and other pagan practices.

Shamballa Bracelets

These bracelets have become very popular in the last few years and have a specific weave and look very pretty. They are associated with Buddhism ideology, and carry spiritual dangers. This design is now being used for Rosaries particularly a Decade Bracelet. They often have St. Benedict or Divine Mercy medal attached. Beware when visiting shrines in Ireland or abroad not to buy this type of design. If you have one, it is best to destroy it.

Because of the lack of teaching from the bible and our catechism, most Catholics are not aware of the dangers by encountering false gods, objects and practices associated with these religions. They have become part of our culture. It's not unusual to have a picture or statue of a Buddha or Hindu god or goddesses in your house as they often symbolise peace and tranquility.

These practices, statues and different ways of life don't bring blessing and have a hidden force that can affect us. You don't need to practice any of these religions to be affected by them. Our God is a Jealous God, a *legitimate* jealously based on his love for us. If you love someone deeply and they turn away from you after everything you have done for them that is legitimate jealously. Christians have been granted many blessings from our God but we often fail to see them and don't realise that they are breaking the first commandment, "I am the Lord your God, '*You shall have no other gods before* **Me**.' From the beginning to the end of the Old Testament, God continually warned the Jewish people in every generation, out of love and concern to refrain from the practices and worship of false gods. Our God, knew that they wouldn't bring blessing to their lives as many of them involved evil practices including human sacrifice and worshiping statues, idols and objects. The widow of Zarephath is very aware that the sins of the past and the practice of idol worship caused her son's death. Elijah restores life to her son and she realises that there is only one true God (1 Kings 17)

Initially our Jewish ancestors were exposed to the gods of Egypt and Canaan, where they lived. As time progressed they were influenced by the gods of the invading empires such as the Assyrians, Babylonians, Greeks and Romans. Jesus then came to heal, teach and deliver the Jews from these influences, so that they could return to a life of blessing. He didn't come to create a new religion. *He came to extend the same blessing that was initially given to the Jews, to ALL nations, so everyone in the world could have blessed lives, because everyone belongs to Him. - [Ezekiel 18:4]* When the Jewish people rejected the teaching of Jesus the small group of Jewish people following the teachings of Jesus had to separate and eventually became Christians. Through the expeditions of St Paul, God's blessing extended initially into the Roman Empire by the 4th century. Since then, the Christian message and God's blessing has reached many parts of the world today and is now the largest religion in the world, however there are many countries who haven't moved forward from old practices, false gods and beliefs. God wants to bring his blessing to all souls on earth. We must follow the Christian message to love and respect our neighbours in all countries of the world, **but not to follow their ways or practices. Gods warnings from over 3000 ago is the same day.**

The disguises of evil has been a pervading problem in every generation and in our time the influences are coming from eastern practices, such as Buddhism, Hinduism, Taoism or ancient Satanic practices that become resurrected and disguised under a new name etc. Many of these practices have common beliefs with Christianity, such as love, respect, peace, be non-judgmental, compassionate etc., but they are not of the spirit of God and contain hidden forces that bring problems, health or otherwise. Have you noticed that many of these countries are truly beautiful and the people are beautiful looking, are so pleasant, have lovely dispositions and attitude, but they are not blessed. The people live in poverty, with poor infrastructures, oppressive governments with little security, education or basic needs etc.; just like the Jews before God answered their prayer and freed them from the Egyptians. God wants to free these people from oppression so they can have a life of abundance, good health, security and freedom.

Buddhism in particular is an atheistic religion and doesn't believe that wrong action has an effect on either the person themselves or others (sin). Therefore it doesn't understand the need to atone for sin or an almighty creator who brings blessing. Buddhists believe that they have to go through cycles of life, death and rebirth until the receive Nirvana (a transcendent state where there is no suffering and heightened wisdom or self-enlightenment). Christians don't realise that they have been handed Nirvana or 'heaven' on a plate on the day of their baptism! It is Gods desire that you return to him in heaven. He provides us with a way of life and wisdom to do so from the bible, and graces and blessings from the sacraments to help us enlighten our souls and free us from suffering even while we are still in the world! If we only knew how much we are blessed but sadly many fundamental church teachings have been lost down through the centuries. Thankfully the Vatican are currently making great strides to re-educate the people of God. In May 2016 the CONGREGATION FOR THE DOCTRINE OF THE FAITH, at the Vatican, released the Letter *"Iuvenescit Ecclesia* **(The Church Rejuvenates)"** to the Bishops of the Catholic Church Regarding the Relationship between Hierarchical and Charismatic Gifts in the Life and the Mission of the Church[4]

The introduction states that it is now more than ever necessary to recognize and value the numerous charisms capable of reawakening and nourishing the life of faith of the People of God. The document continues to encourage us to understand that they are not, therefore, simply human capacities, but are divine in origin, "manifestations of the Spirit" (1 Cor 12:7). We are enlightened by real higher spiritual truths not only for ourselves but to others too. Charisms or gifts such as knowledge, wisdom, prophecy, healing, tongues, miracles are given for the building up of the individual and the people of God as a whole across the world in our daily lives. How amazing would it be, if each Christian opened their heart to the manifestation to the Spirit of God in their lives. Not only would the individual be changed but the world itself would come to understand the power of the mysteries of the Christian Faith and we would all be living heaven on earth!

Replace Meditation for Adoration
Instead of emptying your mind, open your mind and fill your heart and mind with graces and blessings from the direct presence of Jesus. Jesus speaks to us in Adoration. The Vatican *"Letter To The Bishops Of The Catholic Church On Some Aspects Of Christian Meditation"*[5] is very useful in helping us discern the differences between Christian prayer and prayer from other religions.

Replace higher consciousness by calling on the Holy Spirit for wisdom.
If you are a baptised Christian, you in fact already have the Holy Spirit in you, all you need to do is activate it by prayer and you have full access to the almighty spirit of God who wants you to have a full life of blessing, understanding and abundance. Life in the Spirit seminar's are very powerful events and provide an avenue to activating charismatic gifts. All you have to do is ask God with an open heart!

Enlightenment to the truth comes from God.
He has a plan for your life and a path for you that brings blessing. When you align yourself with this you are allowing Gods will and purpose for your unique life to be fulfilled.

What should we do?
When visiting countries that still carry out pagan practices or worship false gods, be sure to;
- Say a prayer of protection every day to block any evil influence you might unknowingly encounter. Likewise call on the precious blood of Jesus every day to cover and protect you during your trip.
- Don't allow anyone to pray with you, even in gratitude.
- Don't take part in any native ceremonies, blessings or rituals. If you have taken part in any non-Christian ceremony, seek out a priest in the deliverance ministry when you get home and ask them to clear any effects that you might have picked up.
- Remove any statues or pictures from your house to a bin then sprinkle Holy Water and Blessed Salt around your house to bless it from any effects or residue from these objects
- I strongly urge you to try to find a catechism or bible course that provide you with the basic teaching of salvation history, so we can attain greater understanding of God and wisdom to help us cope with the trials and tribulations of our daily lives.
- Join a prayer group that is bible based and/or charismatic in nature to allow you to be open to the power of the Holy Spirit.

Sacrifice Sites

I have had a number of experiences in the last few years with people whose houses are built on sacrifice sites. The sites mostly seem to be about 16 feet in diameter. However, in England, there was a site under the aisle of a church which was 12ft wide. About eight or nine people would be involved and a sacrifice of some description would be involved e.g. an animal or human. Whether the house was wholly or partially built on a site, then the family would be affected. The new house would often encounter an uneasy feeling, foul smells, people appearing (lost souls), disturbances etc. In another case, a cattle-shed was built on a site and the owner was physically affected every time they walked in to it. A deliverance ceremony and Mass of the Precious Blood were carried out in all situations to clear the evil and all activity successfully ceased.

In my experience, most of these sacrifices originate from the 14th & 15th century. As of yet, I haven't encountered any from a more recent period. In the last few months alone I have had calls from Down (2), Clare, Kilkenny (2), Cork (2), Kerry, Donegal, Westmeath and Galway. The most active one I encountered was in Co Down a few years ago as follows:

Family Home built on Sacrifice Site
I was contacted by Fr. John from Co. Down in August 2005. A parishioner was having a serious problem in their new family home (parents and five children). On St Stephen's Day 2004, someone visiting the house saw a 'strange female figure' appearing in the house. A few days later, this figure 'appeared' again. Not long afterwards, a man started to appear dressed as a monk in a black habit and always with his head down. They both continued to appear regularly (mostly around 4pm) in the bedrooms, kitchen, outside the house and all members of the family had seen them at one point or another. Once, while one of the children was doing his homework, the kitchen table suddenly shot across the floor and left a scribble across his copy book. They used to have a prayer meeting every week with the bible displayed on a stand. The bible would regularly fly off the stand on to the floor, to be replaced again by the family. Their two-year-old was put to bed but was found on the landing in the morning. Their 12-year-old went to bed as usual one night and also woke up on the landing and didn't know how he got there. Incidents like these happened regularly and the family were so scared, that they would leave the house and on one occasion they stayed with friends for a whole week. Fr. John was very concerned about this family and asked the father to ask the 'figure' who he was and what he wanted. When the figure next appeared he was asked who he was, but the figure gave no reply. When the figure was asked what he wanted, he replied, 'I want you'! Fr. John contacted his bishop and several Masses were celebrated in the house. The situation would temporarily improve, but would then start all over again. I prayed with Fr. John and was directed through Our Lady that evil was at

play. Through further prayer, I was told that the house was built on a sacrifice site that was used over 400 years ago. The two people appearing were part of a group of 9-10 local people who were involved in Satanic sacrifice at this site and were now lost souls. It was decided that a deliverance ceremony would be carried out. In preparation for this, a novena of 9 Masses was celebrated and Fr. John also prayed The Stations of the Cross with the family each night during the novena. Others prayed too. A priest in the deliverance ministry and I travelled to Co. Down in mid October 2005. Mass and a deliverance ceremony were performed in the afternoon and the following day a further ceremony was carried out. The lady stopped appearing after the ceremony and up to December 2005, there was no further disturbance. The 'monk' started to reappear occasionally, but didn't cause any upset like before. Several deliverance Masses were celebrated and this cleared 95% of the problem. In May 2006 the parents came with us to Medjugorje. They both climbed Mount Krezevac in offering for this situation and the father actually climbed everyday in his bare feet and twice on some days for this situation to clear. When they came back there was no further disturbance and everything has been fine since. The penance involved in climbing the mountain, cleared the last 5% of the remaining evil.

Sadly, there is evidence that the practice of offering live animal sacrifices are still in existence in society today.

Evil Spirits are Contagious

Spirits that attach

Michelle was working in Belgium and became sick. Doctors could find no reason for her sicknesses and as her health got worse, she had no choice but to give up her job and move home to Ireland in 2015. She came to visit me and when I prayed about it, I was directed that she was affected by a male co-worker. After we prayed about the co-worker, I was directed that he acquired a spirit of evil by meeting someone involved in evil practices during a trip to Germany. **Spirits can attach themselves and can transfer from person to person**. So in this instance, Michelle in turn was affected after he returned to work. We prayed together and taught her to pray the prayers of protection in the back of the book and she has improved greatly since.

Nigerian Priest in Seminary

I was contacted by Fr Thomas, who was teaching in a seminary in Nigeria. He rang to say that he found it very difficult to cope with the heat in the seminary. I found this strange as he was born in Nigeria and would have been used to the hot climate there. After we prayed I discovered that he was being affected by three of his students. Their families had been involved in witchcraft and that in turn was affecting him. He arranged for a deliverance ceremony to be carried to solve the situation, and the problem stopped after that. **We can get easily affected by people who have been in contact with evil**.

Displaced Furniture

Vivienne was living in Australia in an apartment for a few years and found it very comfortable. After 5 years she noticed that the furniture seemed to move its place. Every morning the furniture was in a different place to the night before, even the patio furniture outside. This really startled her. During a trip home to Ireland in 2015 she came across this book and felt she needed to speak to me. It was going to be difficult as she was flying back the following day, but I managed to fit her in. When we prayed, it was revealed that a new tenant had moved in close to her. The new tenant was involved in some satanic practice and was affecting her situation. She was to have masses of deliverance offered to block the effects. **Here we can see that spirits can move from place to place**.

Foul Smell in House

Testimony from Gerry Maher

I had a tenant living in my house and when he left there was a terrible stench in his room. I cleaned out the room and aired it, but couldn't get rid of it. I tried various cleaners on the floorboards in case something spilled, but the smell was still there. Neighbours offered all sorts of advice and nothing seemed to work. I visited friends and was telling my dilemma. They said I should contact a man called Larry Cummins as it sounded very unusual. I rang Larry and he prayed with me over the phone. He seemed to be having a bad reaction. He told me that my tenant, who was a paramedic, was treating a man in an accident one day. The man was from an eastern religion (non-Christian) which had it's origins in the occult. I was told that the evil spirit that was attached to him, transferred to my tenant and hence the smell in his bedroom. Larry gave me the number of a local priest that deals with these sorts of things. I contacted him and he prayed with me over the phone that evening to clear the smell and to protect me from it again. I'm not religious and don't go to mass, but it's amazing, the smell really is now gone – Gerry Maher, Tipperary

Possessed by a Neighbour

James started seeing a girl, and not too long into the relationship he started to notice that she had certain powers. This included mind reading and being able to control his heart beat and breathing. One evening she moved his jacket along the floor by the power of her mind. His girlfriend often went to fortune tellers and was involved in spiritual practices. She also went through periods of depression and couldn't leave the house. James wore a Benedict Cross around his neck and got concerned by some of the things she was doing one evening. When he took out the cross from under his clothes, she lost her powers. She was really surprised and said 'you've blocked me'. Another time he prayed St Michael the Archangel and again she instantly became blocked. If they went to Mass, she would shake and become affected at the consecration. These powers started to leave James feeling very tired and depressed any time she used them on him. He told me about his situation and I knew by the sound of it, that it was an evil situation that needed to be cured. I contacted Larry who was able to see that this evil had come from a neighbour who lived close by to the girl many years ago. She had been affected from a very young age. She said throughout her life she would have noticed that things would have been going very well for a while and then everything would have come crashing down.

I then put her in contact with Peter in the deliverance ministry as he was more able to deal with this situation than I. Peter said prayers over the phone and removed the 'demon'. Everything seemed to be going well for a couple of weeks until she started to feel bad again. Now she was contemplating suicide. Peter confirmed that this was the effect of the demon resisting the prayer to oust him. I suggested she go see Peter in person. Peter felt the previous situation was cured but he could feel that there was something else tormenting her. He pinpointed that she was abused as a child and this situation was also causing her distress. This is to be looked after professionally. Billy Jones, Northern Ireland

Supermarket Cashier

Testimony from Sally Smith

I went to our local supermarket to do the weekly shopping. When I came to the checkout desk the cashier was a non-national lady. I felt a bit uncomfortable as she had two big bright eyes and kept staring at me. I went home, and had a shower but when I got out of the shower I noticed that my two eyes were very red and my face seemed puffed up. I didn't know what had happened to me. I went to my sister's house to a mass that night. Everyone was asking what had happened to my face and I didn't have an answer for them. During the Mass, the children were particularly disruptive, which was unusual and people in general seemed very uncomfortable and not at ease. I contacted Larry and through prayer he was directed that it I was affected by the lady at the checkout, as she was involved into something of an evil nature. I made contact with two priests the following day. Both prayed with me and my face returned to normal. Larry suggested that I avoid going to that checkout and to say a prayer of protection before entering that supermarket to avoid being affected again. Sally Smith, London

His wife lost her voice

Sean called me as his wife had lost her voice, got physically ill, lost her energy and spent a lot of time in hospital. She went through various medical tests but they proved inconclusive. In Knock in 2009, a lady approached me and explained that she was from the same town and knew of the situation. She said she was with the family on a days outing and noticed a stranger put her arms around the wife twice. Unknown to them, this stranger was dealing in the occult. The church authorities were contacted.

Computer Virus

Joe called me as there was an issue in their company with one of the diagnostic machines in their lab. It was brand new and cost a lot of money. The software failed to read the results or would freeze and then it eventually became corrupt and essential data was lost. The suppliers detected that a virus caused the problem but when a replacement machine was put in place, similar issues happened. After we prayed, it was revealed that a work colleague of Joes had been to a fortune teller and the evil spirit they picked up there came with him to his work place. Joe sprinkled Holy Water and Blessed Salt around the lab and prayed the prayers of protection in the back of this book, to block any spirits that attached to Joe when he came to work. Once this happened, suddenly everything settled down and the machine started working perfectly. A similar issue happened with equipment in another company however in this case the supplier of the equipment to the company was involved in pornography. The evils that were being cause by his actions, was having an effect on the equipment going to the customers!

Testimony from Susie

My daughter loves going to school and always has but one morning last year we got to the school gates and she started crying saying she didn't want to go in. I told her to stop being silly and get into school. I collected her that evening no problem and when I asked how her day was she said 'good'.

The following week the same thing happened every morning but she was getting more and more hysterical and wanted me to stay with her until one morning I took her into her class room screaming and crying. I left the school, walked up the road and got back into my car. Just as I pulled out, she ran out of the school and ran up the road pleading to get into the car. I took her back to school and spoke to the teacher but they didn't know why she was acting this way and told me maybe it was for attention.

I knew something wasn't right, as this was so out of character for her. I contacted Larry and we prayed into the situation. A little boy sitting beside her in class was affecting her, as his family was into black magic.

We had to pray and get a priest in the deliverance ministry to block anything coming from this boy. When I spoke to the teacher the following day it emerged that the boy had just swapped seats before this started. My daughter has no problem going to school anymore. Susie O'Mahony

There has been about 11 situations like this were children are affected by others involved in evil.

Visit to a White Witch

I know of another girl Sarah, who went to a White Witch in Cork for fortune telling. Unknown to her, she brought back a spirit with her. It didn't seem to affect her, but it transferred to her sister Joan. In her sister's work place, the office equipment would breakdown regularly and Joan had a very bad car accident herself and spent a lot of time in rehabilitation. Little did Sarah know doing 'something for fun' could cause so many problems. A Mass of deliverance was celebrated to block the evil. Once this happened, the machines returned to normal, without maintenance being involved.

Nurse affected by the baby she was caring for

Testimony from Sheila Thornton

My experience started when I was looking after a little girl at work who was 10 months old and had been in hospital from birth. While I stood at her cot carrying out some nursing cares, I felt something jump on my back. It felt like two claws digging into my shoulders but it was a fleeting moment and thought nothing more of it.

I spoke to Larry then some months later because I had a feeling of being followed and when I tried to ignore the feeling it just became stronger to the point where I couldn't ignore it anymore. I was also having a lot of trouble sleeping and when I did sleep, I'd just have nightmares and pain in my right shoulder.

I prayed with Larry and he thought the parents of the little girl had been into the occult or were seeing a spiritualist. He recommended I attend a night of deliverance and healing that was taking place in our local church that week.

The priest asked me about the little girl and prayed with me for release of whatever was attached to me. I left the altar and went back to my seat. I started to feel really sick, so got up and went outside for air. I felt better and came back in to the church & started to feel sick again so went back outside for air again, but this didn't help.

The priest came back down to see me and prayed with me for a long time but had to ask Larry to come and help as whatever was there just didn't want to go! It was the strangest feeling. A feeling of something trying to hold on and the efforts and persistence of the prayers it took for me to feel its release.

I was exhausted after the experience and a couple of nights later I was still having nightmares and could see dark shapes swimming in front of my eyes so my mum and dad went back down to the priest to have a mass celebrated for me. After that everything cleared.

The little girl that I'd been looking after had been ready to go home but kept getting infections which meant we couldn't send her home. Surprisingly, not long after my clearance, the little girl's infections cleared up and she was discharged from hospital! Sheila Thornton, London.

Possessed by praying with someone who was possessed!
Monica from Sligo is very devout and goes to a regular prayer group. One evening she told Richard, another member that she felt she was possessed for 20 years. Richard contacted me as he was concerned about the effect it would have on their prayer group. I spoke to Monica and she said that approx 20 years ago, she was praying with someone who was possessed and in turn, she became possessed. The woman told Monica she was possessed, but Monica thought she could pray against it to help the lady. She was completely naive of all that's involved in this ministry and now they were both possessed. This was confirmed to me. I found it amazing that she knew all these years and didn't do anything about it! The demon had been moving around in her body all that time, even at night when she was in bed. A few days later, Richard arranged with Monica to visit a priest in the deliverance ministry. She was a new woman the next day! Everything was gone.

Be careful who you pray with and be careful who you allow to pray with you! Be extremely careful of anyone who lays hands on you unless you know they have been blessed with spiritual gifts from the Holy Spirit.

What can we do to prevent ourselves being affected by evil?
I cannot stress enough the need to say the Prayer of Protection for Freedom from Curses & Evil or St Michael's prayer every day, especially if you have an active prayer life. Satan sees you as a threat and will try to attack you any way he can. On a daily basis, we could be encountering any number of people. We don't know what goes on in their lives or what they are involved in, so it's important to protect yourself. If you are meeting someone whom you know is involved in spiritual practices, say a protection pray before meeting them. For our physical wellbeing, we wash our hands daily to protect ourselves against picking up germs and dirt. We should do the same to protect our spiritual wellbeing.

Spiritual Attacks

Plagued by Despair

Testimony from Robert Gillespie

Last year (2010) I went through a stage where everything seemed to be negative. Where I work, I felt as if bad things were going to happen in the workplace or that I was going to be attacked. I also believed that my wife was going to leave me. When I'd go to bed, I'd try to go to sleep, but my mind was flooded by negative thoughts, a real sense of despair. I couldn't get to sleep, my mind was racing. To me, it seemed that nothing good was happening; it was like I could see no positive outcome to anything. This was going on for about two weeks and I hadn't slept properly at all during this time. I told my wife and she said that I might be under attack. She tried to contact a priest she knew who could pray with me over the phone but he wasn't in. Then she suggested we call Larry. He said to pray the prayer of protection in the back of his book, Please! Pray For Us...We Need Your Help – the Souls in Purgatory. We both prayed it that night and it was the first night's sleep I'd had in two weeks. All my negative thoughts disappeared too. We continue to say this prayer, St Michael's prayer and a prayer to our Guardian Angel every night before we go to bed. Robert Gillespie, Wexford.

Bullied at Work

I met Stephen at a talk in November 2015. He was in his mid 50's and was being bullied by his boss, Sarah. He told me that she was completely irrational, created scenarios that would make it look like he was in the wrong and was very domineering and disrespectful towards him. She was also in the process of suing him. He was very depressed and felt suicidal. I asked him to simply pray the St Michael prayer and customise it for his situation, so that any time he was in the office he could pray it.

St. Michael the Archangel, defend me from any conflict or evil influence coming from my boss Sarah. Be my safeguard against the wickedness and snares of the devil, coming through Sarah my boss. May God restrain him we humbly pray and do thou oh prince of the heavenly host, by the power of God thrust down to hell Satan and with him all the other wicked spirits who wander through this world for the ruin of souls.

He noticed a dramatic improvement very quickly when he started doing this. Sarah never progressed with the threat to sue him and her temperament mellowed towards him. He has more confidence now and is much more at peace and happier in work. I recommend customising the St. Michael prayer for your own situation as it's very powerful.

Despair after getting Engaged

Testimony from Geraldine Jennings

After we got engaged, we went to tell my parents the good news. Everyone was very excited; however about 30 minutes afterwards suddenly I became overwhelmed with a great sense of despair and felt I'd made the wrong decision. Now I was felt trapped as we'd just told everyone. We all went to the pub to 'celebrate'. I put on my smiley face, but my heart was in the depths of despair. This lifted somewhat the following day (Sunday) and I felt somewhat content. The following morning I was going to work and was thinking about what I'd say to break the news to everyone. Suddenly this negative feeling enveloped me again. When I noticed it a second time, I was wondering if I was under spiritual attack. I prayed St Michael's prayer and after I recited it the third time, all the negativity lifted. My heart now felt full of joy. I felt assured I hadn't made a mistake as I figured something good must be happening in our relationship if Satan felt threatened by it! We are now married over four years. Geraldine Jennings, Galway.

Fearful Thoughts almost caused a Mental Breakdown

Testimony from Liz McCarthy

One evening I was at home in the kitchen and out of nowhere I suddenly started having very fearful and intense thoughts. They raced through my mind at speed, telling me that I was going to lose my job and that the projects I was working on were going to fail. I felt completely overwhelmed, insecure and I thought I was going to have a mental breakdown, they were so incessant. I recognised that I was under spiritual attack and started praying the prayer of protection in the back of Larry's book. The thoughts were still very persistent. I prayed St Michael's Prayer and then called on Jesus to cover me in his Precious Blood and continued to say the name of Jesus. The situation eased about 80%, but the experience left me very shaken. I was going out of my mind. Luckily Mass was starting in our local church in 30 minutes and I felt a huge desire to get there ASAP. At the consecration, I placed myself in the chalice and asked Jesus to cover me again in his precious blood and the remaining effects started to clear. After I received communion, the effects finally cleared. Liz McCarthy, Kerry.

The experiences that Robert, Geraldine and Liz had were not their real thoughts and luckily they realised that something more was going on. Without awareness or prayers of protection, people could be led to having breakdowns or committing suicide. In Robert's case, he thought his wife was going to leave him. Satan is trying to break up marriages and creating situations that are not real. If you are having difficulties in your marriage, it's so important call down the graces and blessings that you received from your Sacrament of Marriage to guide, direct, and protect your relationships daily.

Suicidal - Midlands

Stephen visited me from the midlands in February 2016 as he was very agitated and felt suicidal. I prayed a lot with him for his protection. I was very concerned for him as he was in such a state, he was likely to take his own life on the way home. I asked him if he attended mass, confession or prayed and he mentioned that he didn't. We prayed together and I encouraged him to return to Mass. He went the following morning to mass and confession and had a transforming experience. He got in the car and travelled down to me straight away. He was like a new man! He had a radiant look on his face which was so different from the day before and all negative thoughts were gone.

Satan has the ability to influence our thoughts. When we are feeling down, fearful, anxious or negative in ourselves, Satan is influencing our thoughts. He plants voices in our mind that say things like, "I'm no good", "this isn't going to work out", "there's no hope", "I can't see any other way". These thoughts are not your own and they are not from God. After love, the next greatest theme in the bible is fear. Fear has the ability to destroy us. Through the old and new testament, God continually encourages us from the bible "Do not fear", "Do not be afraid". St Pauls echos this in his letter to the Philippians saying that we are to cast out all negative thoughts, because he knows from his own experience that they are not from God! He came under a lot of spiritual attack, so he should know. We don't realise that the full outpouring of the spirit of God and his blessings heal and deliver us through the sacraments.

Father appears to her

Mary called me to say that since her father died, he has been appearing to her. He seemed to come to her when she was in trouble or couldn't cope with life. This has continued for many years. He would often give advice or make her aware of things that needed doing. The last time her dad appeared, he was offering advice that was causing huge problems between Mary and her husband, to the point where they nearly split up. She called me as things had got completely out of hand. I was directed that, it wasn't her dad (this time) but Satan in disguise had been visiting her and was causing all the problems. She arranged a mass to block any evil influences coming in their marriage and all the problems have stopped since.

Suffering Spiritual Attacks because he wasn't baptised

Eric came to visit me unexpectedly one day. He had travelled the whole way from Mayo to our home in north Kilkenny and was very anxious to speak to me. For most of his life he had felt that he was being affected by evil or was possessed. He sought help from three different priests who prayed with him, but he didn't feel any different. He tended to keep to himself as he was concerned that he was affecting the people he came in contact with. I prayed with him and it didn't seem that he was involved in any occult practices, had met anyone involved in occult practices or was possessed. He was a very nice young man and was originally born in the UK. We chatted further and he told me that there were five in his family, three were baptised, however himself and another sibling had not been baptised. Their mother was catholic but lost her faith and fell away from the church before they were born. His dad was not catholic. I was immediately directed that this was the reason why he was feeling the effects of evil around him. I directed him to go to a priest in the deliverance ministry and to also go back to one of the priests he had already met, to get baptised and to keep himself protected.

Eucharistic Minister being Blocked
Nadine is a Eucharistic minister however at some point couldn't bring herself to go to Mass to carry out her duties. Every time she offered to join the roster for Mass, she felt blocked and obstacles kept coming in her way. I suggested she say the pray of protection from Curses & Evil and after that it seemed to clear any effects that were blocking her from carrying out her duties.

Hubcaps causing problems in Laois
Fidelma called me. She had been driving along the road earlier that day and suddenly something took control of the car. She tried to stop the car but it went over a ditch. Luckily she wasn't injured. While we were praying, I was directed that there was something evil connected with the car. After we chatted, and prayed, I was directed that it related to the hubcaps. Her husband had a young man working with him who had taken a liking to the hubcaps. The husband agreed to swap them. Through prayer I was directed that the hubcaps had previously been stolen but nothing got to do with the young man. The husband quickly swapped back the hubcaps and there hasn't been any problem since!

Uninvited Guest in Apartment on Holidays
Testimony from Marian Foley
I was away on holidays in Spain with my husband. We rented a small apartment that had a bedroom upstairs. One night, when we went to bed my husband nodded off, but I was awake for a bit. While I was lying there, I became very aware of an evil spirit in the apartment down stairs. I sensed it coming up the stairs and into our bedroom. I felt it lie on our bed. I was very anxious and started shaking. I said the prayer to St Michael but it didn't go away, so I said an Our Father and then a Hail Mary. As soon as I started praying the Hail Mary, it disappeared. Our Lady to the rescue! Marian Foley, Cork

We forget sometimes in times of spiritual danger that Our Lady is our greatest intercessor before God.

What should we do prevent spiritual attacks

Pray a daily prayer of protection and wear a cross, blessed medal etc
We as humans have **full control** of our thoughts, so let's become more aware of them.

- Negative thoughts – From God or from Satan?
- I can't do this – From God or from Satan?
- We are going to lose everything – From God or Satan?
- We won't be able to cope –From God or Satan?
- Worry, depression, anxiety – From God or Satan?
- I am suicidal – From God or Satan?

Jesus said 'I came so that you could have life and have it to the full'. Jesus doesn't want us to be miserable. Jesus wants us to have joy in our hearts. He wants to free us from bondage of evil.

Since the beginning of time there have always been two worlds – the physical world and the spiritual world. As the physical world has evolved, people have become more grounded in the material things of life and over the centuries, particularly the last century, have gradually forgotten about the spiritual world that surrounds us.

The spiritual world is broken in to two worlds – the world of God and the world of Satan. Both worlds have an influence on our lives and our thoughts.

Everything we do...every decision we make and thought we think, no matter how small, boils back to either a decision to love (from God) or a feeling of fear (Satan). Based on that knowledge we can always confirm the source of our decision. If you ask yourself, why am I doing this, you will soon get the answer, it will be because of a desire to do something good (love) or are we ultimately afraid of something (fear).

If we find that most of our decisions are because of fear, then we are allowing Satan to have a bigger influence over our lives instead of God. We can combat this by saying a prayer of protection from evil and putting our trust in God as He is our creator. God will bring peace to the situation, if you call on him. Compared to the might of the Empire State Building (Jesus), Satan is merely the size of a stinging ant. Yes, he will sting, but Jesus will clear the effect.

The Deliverance Ministry

People and priests in the deliverance ministry need to spend a lot of time in prayer. On a number of occasions I was directed by Our Lady to advise different priests to spend more time in adoration to keep their 'spiritual basket' full.

I know of one official exorcist who prayed with people but his 'spiritual basket' was empty and the deliverance was ineffective. He was very busy, needed a break and wasn't getting sufficient time to pray. Subsequently, the people who needed deliverance came back to me to say the problem was still occurring. I was confused and after I prayed about it, was told the above.

A priest ideally needs to work with someone with the gift of discernment if they don't have it themselves, in order to be guided in what they are doing, whether the situation is cleared or if it needs more prayer.

When celebrating a deliverance ceremony, it is so important to specify the **'exact intention'** that is being prayed for. I know people who have gone to a deliverance ceremony, but the problems continued afterwards, because the priest didn't mention the reason (the specific problem) why the mass was being celebrated. When they went back again and included the intention for the mass, the problems stopped!

My good friend, Fr John Horan from Scartaglen, Co Kerry passed away in October 2010. He delivered many situations and got great satisfaction when people were helped. He was a living saint and believed in the power of prayer and blessed Eucharist to solve everything. He always carried the blessed Eucharist in a miniature monstrance in his inside pocket. When he was praying with someone, he gave them the blessed Eucharist to hold against their chest. When he started to pray with them, I could sense a spiritual wave flashing through their chest and out their back. This was the power of the Holy Spirit working in this person.

Many priests wouldn't be familiar with the discernment or the deliverance ministry as it is not taught in the seminaries.

In England, they have a very good system for dealing with deliverance. Sadly, in Ireland there is nothing organised at church level to deal with these situations. In former days, there was at least one priest in each diocese who was appointed and trained to deal with evil situations. It wasn't publically known but was always there when needed. A priest in this ministry has to go to Rome to be trained, have a great commitment to prayer and have a support group to help. Because of the increase in evil in Ireland this is very serious. It is my understanding that there isn't even one priest in Ireland who operates in an *official capacity* at this point in time.

Here are testimonies from two people I work with in the deliverance ministry.

Testimony from Parish Priest based in the UK

Shortly after I arrived in my present parish, a young woman asked me to bless a candle for her as her flatmate had put a curse upon her. I agreed to her request but suggested first that she kneel at the altar rail whilst I prayed for her. As I prayed, the mosaic floor began to dance around before my eyes. It was then that I realised I was confronting an evil force.

While nothing in my theological training had prepared me for this kind of ministry I was fortunate in that in my early years as a priest, I served in a parish where the priest held a healing service each week and took me with him when he went to pray for haunted houses. However, it was after my experiences at Medjugorje in 1996 that I began to develop the healing and deliverance ministry. On my very first visit I found myself in a group with Larry Cummins. It was a great education to be with him and learn from him. Since that time Larry has visited our church on an annual basis and has been very helpful to me in my ministry, if additional discernment is needed.

In our multi-cultural, multi-faith society, many have come from lands where they have been accustomed to cursing their enemies or getting a witchdoctor to do so. One man came to me whose uncle was jealous of him and was using magic to bring a curse upon him. He was aware of the time that this curse was being pronounced each day. With prayer, many potentially dangerous situations for him and his family have been averted. It is important to note that he is an active Christian who worships regularly. Without this consistent Christian lifestyle our prayers can only have, at best, a temporary or partial effect.

Another source of spiritual evil is involvement in New Age practices such as yoga, Reiki and other therapies. Often such snares are disguised by the use of names which sound very respectable and many people are caught up in them unaware of what it is they are dealing with.

One lady who had spent over £10,000 on Feng Shui and I Ching wanted to receive the fullness of the Holy Spirit, but was unable to do so until she had repented and renounced these practices and then put out all the books, tapes and paraphernalia involved. When she did so, she experienced great peace and joy. Shortly after this she received a wonderful experience of the Holy Spirit.

Sometimes hospitals, local authorities and even churches promote these practices, often out of ignorance of their true nature. In my own parish, when I first arrived, we had yoga classes in the church hall. It was difficult to confront them head-on as they were part of a programme set by the local college of further education. After prayer however, they left of their own accord.

Now I find myself dealing with people who have been spiritually damaged by those classes. One lady in my congregation came to have prayer for deliverance from the ill-effects of yoga. The transformation in her after prayer was truly astounding. She became happy and was glowing with the warmth of the Holy Spirit; a testimony in itself to the true nature of such teachings. Only Jesus Christ can liberate men and women from the bondage these practices entail.

A more pro-active kind of ministry is when we go on prayer walks with the object of cancelling out evil over the land and bringing God's blessing upon it. Occult activity is often present where natural disasters take place. For example, I prayed over an area which had undergone serious flooding. However, when I started to pray, I encountered a witch who was using magic to invoke the forces of nature. I said a silent prayer in the name of Jesus commanding the evil spirit to leave the hill and take the woman with him. To my amazement, she left! The following year floods came to neighbouring regions but did not affect that area. Such experiences demonstrate that reason and logic do not apply when we are up against disincarnate and malevolent forces.
Parish Priest, UK

Testimony from John Gillespie, Belfast
I have been working in the healing and deliverance ministry since 1995. I first met Larry after he came to our area to give a talk. I had heard of him before that and had been referring people to him for direction, where souls in their ancestry needed to be released. I became aware that the people were subsequently help through Larry's direction. There has never been such a need for deliverance here in Ireland as there is now. In my field, people who come to me with depression, mental illness or psychological problems, often have evil at their root, either something they have got involved in themselves or ancestral (something unsolved that's coming down through the bloodline).

In 2005, a 2☐ year old girl was brought to me as she was diagnosed with a very rare form of arthritis. The arthritis was only in her left knee and two fingers on the left hand, including the ring finger. It didn't appear anywhere else on her body. Medical experts claimed it was a rare condition especially as it was happening in someone so young and was isolated. They prescribed steroids which killed the pain for a few weeks but then the pain came back. A priest recommended the family come to me. I prayed for the child and asked God to show me the root cause of this problem. I was shown a vision of a war scene which happened four generations previous. There was an explosion and a man had his left knee and two fingers blown off. He was killed on the battlefield and didn't forgive those who hurt him. The unforgiveness carried down through his bloodline. We prayed to ask forgiveness for the ancestors' sins and those who caused the explosion. The child was totally healed and six years on is perfectly healthy today.

Two years ago, a man came to me for help as he was hospitalised 38 times over a number of months. He was 6' 2'', was down to 9st weight, suicidal and in a lot of stomach pain. Medical tests proved inconclusive. While I prayed for him I was shown a scene from six generations previous. I saw a bullet being shot from a gun and entering the body. The bullet was fiery-hot. I asked him if he had a sharp burning sensation in his intestine. When I pointed to his stomach he said I was the first person to pinpoint the 'actual' spot where the pain was. His ancestor didn't get to forgive the person who shot them before he died (or his family subsequently) and the effect carried on through the generations. This man had masses celebrated, prayed for his ancestry and forgave on their behalf. The pain subsided considerably but wasn't totally gone. A few more masses were celebrated and the pain left him. He has been perfectly healthy since.

There has been a big increase in the number of people contacting me and it continues to escalate. I get a lot of calls every week. I pray with people and ask God to show me what is not of him. Reiki, New Age practices, and hypnosis – I've been shown that they are not of God and that they need to be repented for before God. People have come to me with cancer, heart conditions, lung conditions, headaches and are being affected by evil knowingly or unknowingly. A lady in her mid twenties came to me as she was getting severe headaches for over a year and a half. She had a four-year-old daughter. All medical tests came up negative. I was shown that she had attended a fortune teller. A demon had entered her and was causing the pain. He was tormenting her, she had thoughts that she would die young and she wouldn't see her child grow up. She had to ask God's' forgiveness for crossing over in to Satan's territory. She has committed spiritual adultery. Once she did that, she became totally healed. It was spiritual problem not a medical one. Where evil has come in through sin, it has to be atoned for.

These sufferings are not caused by God. Some people believe that they have been given a cross that they have to carry or that the suffering is God's' will for them. This is a lie of Satan. There are a small percentage of people who have genuinely been chosen by God for redemptive suffering, however in a lot of cases, 'something' has caused this suffering and it needs to be broken. In cases like these, evil is hidden underneath but God has all the answers to clear it. This is where the gifts of discernment and knowledge, which myself and Larry have, are so important when helping others. God is like a spiritual website with a wealth of information and answers. Through these gifts we have been given the ability to download the answers to help others. It's like we've been given the password to get in!
John Gillespie, Belfast.

SACRAMENTALS – Powerful tools for Protection & Deliverance

Due to the extent of evil harassing us in our daily lives and our modern society, we wish to offer you the following prayers. These exorcism prayers should be recited by a Catholic priest, so take them to your local Catholic priest to have them recited over your container of Salt, Water, Candles, St Benedict Medal/Cross and Brown Scapular.

EXORCISM PRAYERS FOR BLESSING OF SALT AND WATER FROM THE ROMAN RITUAL

1. When you see this symbol '†', make the Sign of the Cross.
2. R: means response and this is what the lay people are to respond.
3. P: means the Catholic priest is to read aloud.

Exorcism of Salt:
P: God's creature, salt, I cast out the demon from you by the Living † God, by the True † God, by the Holy † God, by God who ordered you to be thrown into the water spring by Eliseus to heal it of its barrenness.

May you be a purified salt, a means of health for those who believe, a medicine for body and soul for all who make use of you. May all evil fancies of the foul fiend, his malice and cunning, be driven afar from the place where you are sprinkled. And let every unclean spirit be repulsed by Him who is coming to judge both the living and the dead and the world by fire.
R: Amen.
P: Let us pray, Almighty everlasting God, we humbly appeal to Your mercy and goodness to graciously bless † this creature, salt, which you have given for mankind's use. May all who use it find in it a remedy for body and mind. And may everything that it touches or sprinkles be freed from uncleanness and any influence of the evil spirit; through Christ our Lord.
R: Amen.

Exorcism of Water:
P: God's creature, water, I cast out the demon from you in the name of God † the Living Father Almighty, in the name of Jesus † Christ, His Son, our Lord, and in the power of the Holy † Spirit. May you be purified water, empowered to drive afar all power of the enemy, in fact, to root out and banish the enemy himself, along with his fallen angels. We ask this through the power of our Lord Jesus Christ, who is coming to judge both the living and the dead and the world by fire.

R: Amen.

P: Let us pray, O God, who for man's welfare established the most wonderful mysteries in the substance of water, hearken to our prayer, and pour forth your blessings on this element now being prepared with various purifying rites. May this creature of yours, when used in your mysteries and endowed with your grace, serve to cast out demons and to banish disease. May everything that this water sprinkles in the homes and gatherings of the faithful be delivered from all that is unclean and hurtful; let no breath of contagion hover there, no taint of corruption; let all the wiles of the lurking enemy come to nothing. By the sprinkling of this water may everything opposed to the safety and peace of the occupants of these homes be banished, so that in calling on your holy name they may know the wellbeing they desire, and be protected from every peril; through Christ our Lord.

R: Amen.

Blessed Salt – can be any type of salt that has been blessed by a priest.

Catholic Priest pours the salt into the water in the form of a cross, saying:

P. May this salt and water be mixed together; in the name of the Father and of the Son, † and of the Holy Sprit.

R. Amen.

P. The Lord be with you.

R. May He also be with you.

P. Let us pray: God, source of irresistible might and king of an invincible realm, the ever glorious conqueror; who restrain the force of the adversary, silencing the uproar of his rage, and valiantly subduing his wickedness; in awe and humility we beg you, Lord to regard with favour this creature thing of salt and water, to let the light of your kindness shine upon it, and to hallow it with the dew of your mercy; so that wherever it is sprinkled and your holy name is invoked, every assault of the unclean spirit may be baffled, and all dread of the serpent's venom be cast out. To us who entreat your mercy grant that the Holy Spirit may be with us wherever we may be; through Christ our Lord.

R: Amen.

Christ's faithful are permitted to take holy water home with them to sprinkle the sick, their homes, fields, vineyards and the like. It is recommended too that they put it in fonts in the various rooms of their homes, so that they may use it to bless themselves daily and frequently.

Blessing of Candles

Lord Jesus, You are the Light of the world:
we praise You,
and ask You to guide our steps each day.

Help us to love You and serve You faithfully,
and to carry our daily cross with You.

Bless † this candle,
and let it always remind us
that You are our Light in darkness,
our Protector in danger,
and our saving Lord at all times.

Lord Jesus,
we praise You and give You glory,
for You are Lord for ever and ever. Amen.

Approved Blessing of the Medal of St. Benedict

Medals of Saint Benedict are sacramentals that may be blessed legitimately by any priest or deacon – not necessarily Benedictine (Instr., 26 Sept. 1964; Can. 1168).

P. Our help is in the name of the Lord.
R. Who made heaven and earth.
In the name of God the Father † almighty, who made heaven and earth, the seas and all that is in them, I exorcise these medals against the power and attacks of the evil one. May all who use these medals devoutly be blessed with health of soul and body. In the name of the Father † almighty, of the Son † Jesus Christ our Lord, and of the Holy † Spirit the Paraclete, and in the love of the same Lord Jesus Christ who will come on the last day to judge the living and the dead, and the world by fire. Amen.

Let us pray. Almighty God, the boundless source of all good things, we humbly ask that, through the intercession of Saint Benedict, you pour out your blessings † upon these medals. May those who use them devoutly and earnestly strive to perform good works be blessed by you with health of soul and body, the grace of a holy life, and remission of the temporal punishment due to sin.

May they also with the help of your merciful love, resist the temptation of the evil one and strive to exercise true charity and justice toward all, so that one day they may appear sinless and holy in your sight. This we ask though Christ our Lord. Amen.

The medals are then sprinkled with holy water. You can use the same wording for blessing St Benedict Crosses.
Permissu superiorum
Nihil obstat and Imprimatur, Saint Cloud, 24 April 1980.

Brown Scapular Blessing and Enrolment

Our Lady gave the Brown Scapular to St. Simon Stock on July 16, 1251. She promised that those who wear it would gain salvation, protection, and peace. In a dream the Blessed Mother appeared to Pope John XXII and said,

'I, the Mother of Grace, shall descend on the Saturday after their death and whomsoever I shall find in Purgatory, I shall free, so that I may lead them to the holy mountain of life everlasting.'

Introductory Prayer
(Priest vests in surplice and white stole)
P: Show us, Lord, thy mercy.
R: And grant us thy salvation.
P: Lord, hear my prayer.
R: And let my cry come unto thee.
P: The Lord be with you.
R: And with your spirit.

Brown Scapular Blessing

P: Let us pray. Lord Jesus Christ, Saviour of mankind, sanctify † by thy power these scapulars, which for love of thee and for love of Our Lady of Mount Carmel, thy servants will wear devoutly, so that through the intercession of the same Virgin Mary, Mother of God, and protected against the evil spirit, they may persevere in thy grace until death. Thou who liveth and reigneth world without end.
R: Amen.
(Priest sprinkles scapulars with holy water and distributes them)

Brown Scapular Confraternity Enrolment (Enrolment is for life)

P: Receive this blessed scapular and beseech the Blessed Virgin, that by her merits, you may wear it without stain. May it defend you against all adversity and accompany you to eternal life.
R: Amen.
P: I, by the power vested in me, admit you to participate in all the spiritual benefits obtained through the mercy of Jesus Christ, by the Religious Order of Mount Carmel. In the name of the Father (†), and of the Son (†), and of the Holy Ghost (†).
R: Amen.
P: May God Almighty, the Creator of heaven and earth, bless you (†); he who has deigned to join you to the Confraternity of the Blessed Virgin of Mount Carmel. We beseech her to crush the head of the ancient serpent, so that you may enter into possession of your eternal heritage. Through Christ our Lord.
R: Amen.☐

Prayers of Protection/Deliverance

The Rosary – Our Lady is the most powerful intercessor

Stations of the Cross
Offer up the sufferings of Jesus on the cross in atonement for an evil situation.

The Divine Mercy

Prayer to St Michael the Archangel
St. Michael the Archangel, defend us in our hour of conflict. Be our safeguard against the wickedness and snares of the devil. May God restrain him we humbly pray and do thou oh prince of the heavenly host, by the power of God thrust down to hell Satan and with him all the other wicked spirits who wander through this world for the ruin of souls.

Before commencing any prayer of deliverance, state out loud the 'specific reason' for the prayer using the following phrase. **"I say this prayer of protection to uproot, destroy, block, seal, bind, break and stop the effects of (name the problem e.g jealously) coming from (name the source..my neighbor Sean)."**

Prayer of Protection for Freedom from Curses & Evil
I place myself in the presence of Jesus Christ and submit to His Lordship. I 'Put on God's armour so as to be able to resist the devil's tactics' (Ephesians 6;10-11). I stand my ground, 'with truth buckled around my waist, and integrity for a breastplate…' (Ephesians 6;14). I carry the 'shield of faith' to 'put out the arrows of the evil one…' (Ephesians 6;16). I accept 'salvation from God to be my helmet and received the word of God from the Spirit to use as a sword' (Ephesians 6:17). In the name of Jesus Christ crucified, died and risen, I bind all spirits of the air, the atmosphere, the water, the fire, the wind, the ground, the underground, and the nether world. I also bind the influence of any lost or fallen souls who may be present, and all emissaries of the Satanic headquarters or any coven of witches or warlocks or Satan worshippers who may be present in some preter-natural way. I claim the blood of Jesus on the air and atmosphere, the water, the fire, the wind, the ground and their fruits all around us, the underground and nether world.

In the name of Jesus Christ I forbid every adversary mentioned to communicate with or help one another in any way, or to communicate with me, or to do anything at all except what I command in Jesus name.

> In the name of Jesus Christ I seal this place and all present and all family and associates of those present and their places and possessions and sources of supply in the blood of Jesus. (Repeat three times)

In the name of Jesus Christ I forbid any lost spirits, covens, Satanic groups or emissaries or any of their associates, subjects or superiors to harm or take revenge on me, my family and my associates, or cause harm or damage to anything we have.

> In the name of Jesus Christ and by the merits of His Precious Blood, I break and dissolve every curse, hex, seal, spell, sorcery, bond, snare, trap, device, lie, stumbling block, obstacle, deception, diversion or distraction, spiritual chain or spiritual influence, also every disease of body, souls, mind or spirit placed upon us, or on this place, or on any of the persons, places and things mentioned, by any agent, or brought on us by our own mistakes or sins. (Repeat three times)

I now place the cross of Jesus Christ between myself and all generations in my family tree. I say in the name of Jesus Christ that there will be no direct communication between the generations. All communications will be filtered through the Precious Blood of the Lord Jesus Christ.

Mary, the Immaculate, clothe me in the light and power of your faith. Father, please assign the angels and saints to assist me. Thank You, Lord Jesus, for being my Wisdom, my Justice, my Sanctification, and my Redemption. I surrender to the ministry of Your Holy Spirit, and receive Your truth concerning intergenerational healing. Glory be to the Father, and to the Son and to the Holy Spirit. As it was in the beginning, is now and ever shall be, world without end. Amen.

Father Robert DeGrandis S.S.J

It is said that the four most powerful words against evil are 'Jesus', 'Mary', 'Precious Blood' and 'the word of God'. The prayer above contains all four and I have found this prayer most effective for dealing with a multitude of situations. The original purpose of this prayer was created for intergenerational healing, however I customise the prayer with as much information as I have to suit the situation and I recommend that you do this too as it has proven very powerful. Include specific names, places, actions as much as possible. It's important to state the *exact issue*, *what* your blocking, and from *who / or as a result of.*

Sample Customised Prayer
"I say this prayer of protection to uproot, destroy, block, seal, bind and break the effects of anger, bitterness, resentment, jealously and hatred coming from my neighbor Sean Flynn, which has affected my livestock and business, as a result of a disagreement we had"

I place myself, *my family, livestock and business* in the presence of Jesus Christ and submit to His Lordship. I 'Put on God's armour so as to be able to resist the devil's tactics' (Ephesians 6;10-11). I stand my ground, 'with truth buckled around my waist, and integrity for a breastplate...' (Ephesians 6;14). I carry the 'shield of faith' to 'put out the arrows of the evil one...' (Ephesians 6;16). I accept 'salvation from God to be my helmet and received the word of God from the Spirit to use as a sword' (Ephesians 6:17). In the name of Jesus Christ crucified, died and risen, I bind all spirits of the air, the atmosphere, the water, the fire, the wind, the ground, the underground, and the nether world *surrounding my farm*. I also bind the influence of any lost or fallen souls who may be present, and all emissaries of the Satanic headquarters or any coven of witches or warlocks or Satan worshippers who may be present in some preter-natural way. I claim the blood of Jesus on the air and atmosphere, the water, the fire, the wind, the ground and their fruits all around us, the underground and nether world, *around my farm*.

In the name of Jesus Christ I forbid every adversary mentioned to communicate with or help one another in any way, or to communicate with me, or to do anything at all except what I command in Jesus name.

> In the name of Jesus Christ I seal *myself, my family, livestock and business* and all present and all family and associates of those present and their places and possessions and sources of supply in the blood of Jesus. (Repeat three times)

In the name of Jesus Christ I forbid any lost spirits, covens, Satanic groups or emissaries or any of their associates, subjects or superiors to harm or take revenge on me, *my family, livestock and business* and my associates, or cause harm or damage to anything we have.

> In the name of Jesus Christ and by the merits of His Precious Blood, I break and dissolve *the effects of anger, bitterness, resentment, jealously and hatred coming from my neighbor Sean Flynn, which has affected my livestock and business, as a result of a disagreement we had* and every curse, hex, seal, spell, sorcery, bond, snare, trap, device, lie, stumbling block, obstacle, deception, diversion or distraction, spiritual chain or spiritual influence, also every disease of body, souls, mind or spirit placed upon us, or on this place, or on any of the persons, places and things mentioned, by any agent, or brought on us by our own mistakes or sins. (Repeat three times)

I now place the cross of Jesus Christ between myself, *my family, livestock and business and the effects of anger, bitterness, resentment, jealously and hatred coming from my neighbor Sean Flynn.* I say in the name of Jesus Christ that there will be *no direct communication between us and all* communications will be filtered through the Precious Blood of the Lord Jesus Christ.

Mary, the Immaculate, clothe *me, my family, livestock and business* in the light and power of your faith. Father, please assign the angels and saints to assist me. Thank You, Lord Jesus, for being my Wisdom, my Justice, my Sanctification, and my Redemption. I surrender to the ministry of Your Holy Spirit, and receive Your truth concerning *this situation*. Glory be to the Father, and to the Son and to the Holy Spirit. As it was in the beginning, is now and ever shall be, world without end. Amen.

Original Prayer to St. Michael The Archangel, against Satan and the Rebellious Angels
Published by the Order of His Holiness Pope Leo XIII.

The term "exorcism" does NOT always denote a solemn exorcism involving a person possessed by the devil. In general, the term denotes prayers to "curb the power of the devil and prevent him from doing harm." As St. Peter had written in Holy Scripture, "your adversary the devil, as a roaring lion, goes about seeking whom he may devour." [1 St.Pet. 5:8]

The Holy Father exhorts priests to say this prayer as often as possible, as a simple exorcism to curb the power of the devil and prevent him from doing harm. The faithful also may say it in their own name, for the same purpose, as any approved prayer. Its use is recommended whenever action of the devil is suspected, causing malice in men, violent temptations and even storms and various calamities. It could be used as a solemn exorcism (an official and public ceremony, in Latin), to expel the devil. It would then be said by a priest, in the name of the Church and only with a Bishop's permission.

Prayer to St. Michael the Archangel
In the Name of the Father, and of the Son, and of the Holy Spirit. Amen.

Most glorious Prince of the Heavenly Armies, Saint Michael the Archangel, defend us in "our battle against principalities and powers, against the rulers of this world of darkness, against the spirits of wickedness in the high places" [Eph., 6:12].

Come to the assistance of men whom God has created to His likeness and whom He has redeemed at a great price from the tyranny of the devil. The Holy Church venerates you as her guardian and protector; to you, the Lord has entrusted the souls of the redeemed to be led into heaven. Pray therefore the God of Peace to crush Satan beneath our feet, that he may no longer retain men captive and do injury to the Church. Offer our prayers to the Most High, that without delay they may draw His mercy down upon us; take hold of "the dragon, the old serpent, which is the devil and Satan," bind him and cast him into the bottomless pit "that he may no longer seduce the nations." [Rev. 20:2-3]

Exorcism

In the Name of Jesus Christ, our God and Lord, strengthened by the intercession of the Immaculate Virgin Mary, Mother of God, of Blessed Michael the Archangel, of the Blessed Apostles Peter and Paul and all the Saints. and powerful in the holy authority of our ministry, we confidently undertake to repulse the attacks and deceits of the devil. God arises; His enemies are scattered and those who hate Him flee before Him. As smoke is driven away, so are they driven; as wax melts before the fire, so the wicked perish at the presence of God.

P. Behold the Cross of the Lord, flee bands of enemies.

R. The Lion of the tribe of Juda, the offspring of David, hath conquered.

P. May Thy mercy, Lord, descend upon us.

R. As great as our hope in Thee.

We drive you from us, whoever you may be, unclean spirits, all satanic powers, all infernal invaders, all wicked legions, assemblies and sects. In the Name and by the power of Our Lord Jesus Christ, † may you be snatched away and driven from the Church of God and from the souls made to the image and likeness of God and redeemed by the Precious Blood of the Divine Lamb †.

Most cunning serpent, you shall no more dare to deceive the human race, persecute the Church, torment God's elect and sift them as wheat.

The Most High God commands you. † He with whom, in your great insolence, you still claim to be equal: "God who wants all men to be saved and to come to the knowledge of the truth." [1 Tim. 2:4)

God the Father commands you. †

God the Son commands you. †

God the Holy Ghost commands you. †

Christ, God's Word made flesh, commands you; †

He who to save our race outdone through your envy, "humbled Himself, becoming obedient even unto death" [Phil. 2:8); He who has built His Church on the firm rock and declared that the gates of hell shall not prevail against Her, because He will dwell with Her "all days even to the end of the world." Mt. 28:20]

The sacred Sign of the Cross commands you, † as does also the power of the mysteries of the Christian Faith. †

The glorious Mother of God, the Virgin Mary, commands you; † she who by her humility and from the first moment of her Immaculate Conception crushed your proud head.

The faith of the holy Apostles Peter and Paul, and of the other Apostles commands you.†

The blood of the Martyrs and the pious intercession of all the Saints command you. †

Thus, cursed dragon, and you, diabolical legions, we adjure you

by the living God, †

by the true God, †

by the holy God, †

by the God "who so loved the world that He gave up His only Son, that every soul believing in Him might not perish but have life everlasting;" [St.Jn. 3:16] stop deceiving human creatures and pouring out to them the poison of eternal damnation; stop harming the Church and hindering her liberty. Begone, Satan, inventor and master of all deceit, enemy of man's salvation. Give place to Christ in Whom you have found none of your works; give place to the One, Holy, Catholic and Apostolic Church acquired by Christ at the price of His Blood.

Stoop beneath the all-powerful Hand of God; tremble and flee when we invoke the Holy and terrible Name of Jesus, this Name which causes hell to tremble, this Name to which the Virtues, Powers and Dominations of heaven are humbly submissive, this Name which the Cherubim and Seraphim praise unceasingly repeating: Holy, Holy, Holy is the Lord, the God of Hosts.

P. O Lord, hear my prayer.

R. And let my cry come unto Thee.

P. May the Lord be with thee.

R. And with thy spirit.

Let us pray.

God of heaven,

God of earth,

God of Angels,

God of Archangels,

God of Patriarchs,

God of Prophets,

God of Apostles,

God of Martyrs,

God of Confessors,

God of Virgins,

God who has power to give life after death and rest after work: because there is no other God than Thee and there can be no other, for Thou art the Creator of all things, visible and invisible, of Whose reign there shall be no end, we humbly prostrate ourselves before Thy glorious Majesty and we beseech Thee to deliver us by Thy power from all the tyranny of the infernal spirits, from their snares, their lies and their furious wickedness.

Deign, O Lord, to grant us Thy powerful protection and to keep us safe and sound. We beseech Thee through Jesus Christ Our Lord. Amen.

P. From the snares of the devil,
R. Deliver us, O Lord.
P. That Thy Church may serve Thee in peace and liberty:
R. We beseech Thee to hear us.
P. That Thou may crush down all enemies of Thy Church:
R. We beseech Thee to hear us.

(Holy water is sprinkled in the place where we may be.)

Some websites state that this prayer should not be prayed by lay people but when discerning whether to include it in this book, Our Lady confirmed that it can be prayed by lay people because of the increase of evil in the world.

Healing of Ancestry – A Prayer of Deliverance

Eternal Father, as a community of faith and a family in prayer, we gather to give you praise, adoration and thanksgiving in all things. We pray for all the deceased members of the families represented here, and all those who, in the past, were born deceased, still born, miscarried, aborted, never committed to God and those who died an early death. We pray for your family members who died brutally or violently, lost in the war or otherwise died from strange and mysterious illnesses, for great fears, acts of cowardice, sudden death, in mysterious fires and for all who were rejected by the family, wanderers and lost members, adopted, abandoned, or rejected.

We pray for all the members of the families represented here who were addicted to drugs, alcohol, games, compulsion of all kinds, gambling, lust, deceitfulness, addictive shopping, and for family members unduly attached to values of the world, money, prestige, power and control over persons or things.

We pray for those who died and were never prayed for and those buried without a proper funeral. We pray for those who died by their own hand and for those who died through suffocation or were abandoned, for those afflicted with great phobias, emotional instability, insanity, unexplained illness and from all other causes known by God alone.

We ask release from all bondage coming from the occult, under any form practiced by family members in the past or in the present affecting living members in whatever negative form of bondage, infirmity, emotional or physical illness, addiction of any kind, spiritual torment or other confusion. I hereby rebuke and cast out in the Name of Jesus Christ, from all living members of these families, the following dark and binding forces of spiritual and emotional torment, undue anxieties, tensions and stress, violence, prejudice, error, devaluation, self-hatred, retaliation, arrogance and deceitful pride in all its forms.

We ask deliverance from fears of all kinds – the fear of being found out, the fear of ghosts, fears of natural elements such as heights, thunder, lightening, wind, water, fire, closed spaces, fearful dreams, the fear of rejection, the fear of intimacy, the fear of failure, the fear of success, the fear of man, the fear of woman, the fear of darkness and all other kinds of fears, spiritual, emotional or physical from whatever source.

I hereby rebuke and cast out, in the name of Jesus Christ all dark and binding forces of superstition, slander, destructive lies, and falsehoods, deception in all its forms and attempts to destroy others' reputation, lust, incest and perversions of all kinds. I hereby rebuke and cast out, in the Name of Jesus Christ obsessive and compulsive destructive behaviour, manic attitudes, depressions, denial and deceitful games, abandonment, rage, excessive anger, guilt, vengeance and self-destructive anxieties, attitudes and attempts.

I hereby rebuke and cast out, in the name of Jesus Christ, the following dark and binding forces called confusion, chaos, rebellion, arrogance, hallucinations, sleep walking, addiction, fortune telling in all its forms, witchcraft, Satanism, necromancy, santeria, black mass, and occultism in all its forms.

In the name of Jesus Christ, I rebuke and cast out all deceitful and destructive forces of despair, betrayal, uncontrolled frustrations, bitterness, despondency, repression, projection in all its forms, manipulation and control, the fear of rejection, self-deceit, rejection and self-rejection, exaggerated anxieties, withdrawal, self-pity, false guilt and perversions of all kinds.

I rebuke and cast out in the name of Jesus Christ, the dark and binding forces of pride, denial fantasies, doubt, mockery, repression, hopelessness, fear of insanity, fear of perdition, infidelity, abuses of all kinds, verbal, mental, emotional, physical or spiritual. I rebuke and cast out in the name of Jesus Christ all false God's and idols.

Seal, I break you in the Name of Jesus Christ
Seal, I break you in the Name of Jesus Christ
Seal, I break you in the Name of Jesus Christ

I hearby break and cast out in the name of Jesus Christ all curses of any kind placed upon the members of the families represented here and all ancestry of these families.

I hearby break and sever by the power of the Word of God and the Sword of the Spirit all negative ancestral spirits and influences of any kind from whatever source, genetic, spiritual, physical, emotional or physic affecting the living members of these families wherever they may now be living.

In the name of all these past and lost or injured souls, I ask forgiveness for those who died unforgiven and unforgiving. For them, we ask deliverance from present darkness, confusion and chaos. As a family, we raise up to God all the ancestors, who were never baptised for whatever reason. We ask the Lord to accept them, through the baptism of desire, in to the family of the church with a right to Heaven. We bestow upon each one of them the name of family members who surrounded them at the time of their death. We command the Holy Angels, in the Name of Jesus Christ, to lead all these souls into Paradise to be forever in the Presence of our heavenly Father, the angels and the saints and from this moment on, to be intercessors for all the living members of the families represented here today. I claim the most Precious Blood of Jesus Christ upon all members of these families, that they be protected from all harm, injury, accident, illness and the wiles of the devil. I also ask the Holy Angels to be, now and always, sentries of protection for all the members of the families represented here today. I ask the angels to protect their possessions from all harm and destructive forces.

We make our prayer in the name of Jesus of Nazareth whose compassionate love heals all wounds through forgiveness, mercy and prayer. AMEN.

Prayer of Forgiveness
The following prayer covers most significant areas of forgiveness. Often, such a prayer will bring to mind other areas that need forgiveness. Let the Holy Spirit move freely and guide your mind to persons or groups that you need to forgive.

Let us pray...
Lord Jesus Christ, I ask today to forgive EVERYONE in my life. I know that You will give me the strength to forgive and I thank You that You love me more than I love myself and want my happiness more than I desire it for myself. Father, I forgive YOU for the times death has come into the family, hard times, financial difficulties,

or what I thought were punishments sent by You and people said, 'It's God's will,' and I become bitter and resentful toward You.

Purify my heart and mind today. Lord, I forgive MYSELF for my sins, faults and failings, for all that is bad in myself or that I think is bad,I forgive myself; and I accept Your forgiveness. I further forgive MYSELF for taking Your name in vain, not worshipping You by attending church, for hurting my parents, getting drunk, for sins against purity, bad books, bad movies, fornication, adultery. Also, for abortion, stealing, lying, defrauding and hurting peoples' reputation. You have forgiven me today, and I forgive myself.

Thank You, Lord, for your grace at this moment. I also forgive MYSELF for any delving in superstition, using ouija boards, horoscopes, going to séances, using fortune telling or wearing lucky charms. I reject all that superstition and choose You alone as my Lord and Saviour. Fill me with Your Holy Spirit.

Lord, I truly forgive my MOTHER. I forgive her for all the times she hurt me, she resented me, she was angry with me and for all the times she punished me. I forgive her for the times she preferred my brothers and sisters to me. I forgive her for the times she told me I was dumb, ugly, stupid, the worst of the children or that I cost the family a lot of money. For the times she told me I was unwanted, an accident, a mistake or not what she expected, I forgive her.

Lord, I truly forgive my FATHER. I forgive him for any non-support, any lack of love, affection or attention. I forgive him for any lack of time, for not giving me his companionship, for his drinking, arguing and fighting with my mother or the other children. For his severe punishments, for desertion, for being away from home, for divorcing my mother or for any affairs, I do forgive him.

Lord, I extend forgiveness to my SISTERS AND BROTHERS. I forgive those who rejected me, lied about me, hated me, resented me, competed for my parents' love, those who hurt me, who physically harmed me. For those who were too severe on me, punished me or made my life unpleasant in any way, I do forgive them.

Lord, I forgive my SPOUSE for lack of love, affection, consideration, support, attention, communication; for faults, failings, weaknesses and those other acts or words that hurt or disturb me.
Jesus, I forgive my CHILDREN for their lack of respect, obedience, love, attention, support, warmth, understanding; for their bad habits, falling away from the church, any bad actions which disturb me.
Lord God, I forgive my IN-LAWS, MY MOTHER-IN-LAW, FATHER-IN-LAW, SON/DAUGHTER-IN-LAW AND OTHER RELATIVES by marriage, who treat my family with a lack of love. For all their words, thoughts, actions or omissions which injure

and cause pain, I forgive them.

Please help to forgive my RELATIVES, my grandmother and grandfather, aunts, uncles, cousins, who may have interfered in our family, been possessive of my parents, who may have caused confusion or turned one parent against the other.

Jesus, help me to forgive my CO-WORKERS who are disagreeable or make life miserable for me. For those who push their work off on me, gossip about me, won't cooperate with me, try to take my job, I do forgive them.

My NEIGHBOURS need to be forgiven, Lord. For all their noise, letting their property run down, not tying up their dogs that run through my yard, not taking in their rubbish bins, being prejudiced and running down the neighbourhood, I do forgive them.

I do forgive my PRIEST, my CONGREGATION and my CHURCH for their lack of support, affirmation, bad sermons, pettiness, lack of friendliness, not providing me or my family with the inspiration we needed, for any hurts they have inflicted on me or my family, even in the distant past, I forgive them today.

Lord, I forgive all those who are of different PERSUASIONS, those of opposite political views who have attacked me, ridiculed me, discriminated against me; made fun of me, economically hurt me.

I forgive those of different religious DENOMINATIONS AND BELIEFS who have harassed me, attacked me, argued with me, and forced their view on me or my family.

Those who have harmed me ETHNICALLY, have discriminated against me, mocked me, made jokes about my race or nationality, hurt my family physically, emotionally or economically, I do forgive them today.

Lord, I forgive all PROFESSIONAL PEOPLE who have hurt me in any way: doctors, nurses, lawyers, judges, politicians and civil servants.

I forgive all service people: policemen, firemen, bus drivers, hospital workers and especially repairmen who have taken advantage of me in their work.

Lord, I forgive my EMPLOYER for not paying me enough money, for not appreciating my work, for being unkind and unreasonable with me, for being angry or unfriendly, for not promoting me, and for not complimenting me on my work.

Lord, I forgive my SCHOOLTEACHERS AND INSTRUCTORS of the past as well as the present. For those who punished me, humiliated me, insulted me, treated me unjustly, made fun of me, called me dumb or stupid, made me stay after school, I truly forgive them today.

Lord, I forgive my FRIENDS who have let me down, lost contact with me, do not support me, were not available when I needed help, borrowed money and did not return it, gossiped about me.

Lord Jesus, I especially pray for the grace of forgiveness for the ONE PERSON in life who has HURT ME THE MOST. I ask to forgive anyone who I consider my greatest enemy, the one who is the hardest to forgive or the one who I said I will never forgive.

Lord, I beg pardon of all these people for the hurt I have inflicted on them, especially my mother and father, and my marriage partner. I am especially sorry for the three greatest hurts I have inflicted on each of these.

Thank You, Jesus, that I am being freed of the evil of unforgiveness.
Let Your Holy Spirit fill me with light and let every dark area of my mind be enlightened. AMEN.

Forgiveness is an act of the will, not a feeling. If we pray for a person, we can be assured that we have forgiven that person. To help accept an individual and open ourselves to a particular person more, picture
him with the Lord Jesus and say to the Lord, 'I love him because You love him. I forgive him because You forgive him.'

Forgiveness is a life-long obligation. Daily we need to forgive those who hurt or injure us.

Father Robert DeGrandis S.S.J

Apology to God Our Father
GOD OUR FATHER. I apologise and ask forgiveness for my sins and the sins of my ancestors and my children's ancestors in my mother's and father's family trees, including...(insert family names).
I apologise for all the anger and unforgiveness, bitterness and resentment, between all members of my family tree. I apologise to God our Father, for all the fighting over land or money, envy and jealousy, blasphemy, corruption, curses, dissension, drunkenness, anti-semitism, hatred, filthy language, lack of faith, unbelief, lying, malice, murder, wrath, rebellion and selfish ambitions.

GOD OUR FATHER, I apologise for any attempted suicide and self destruction, all abortions and assistance in abortions.

GOD OUR FATHER, I apologise for all the ancestors who were involved in war and oppression who may have misused their positions of authority through the power of guns and explosives. I apologise for any involvement in illegal organisations in times of conflict in Ireland. I apologise for any torture or suffering that may have been inflicted on others.

GOD OUR FATHER, I apologise for all addictions, for alcoholism and for any making and selling of illicit alcohol and drugs

GOD OUR FATHER, I apologise and ask forgiveness for sins of immorality, indecency, lust, impurity, rape, incest, bitterness or lack of responsibility in the home, such as deprivation of children, violence both verbal and physical.

GOD OUR FATHER, I apologise for any involvement in the occult, by fortune telling, tea-leaf reading, superstition, horoscope, tarot cards, charms, palmistry, ouija boards, spiritualism, witchcraft, black magic, white magic, domination, black mass, crystal ball reading, divination, extra sensory perception

GOD OUR FATHER, I apologise for any perjury, pride, dishonesty, gluttony, insincerity, cheating for gain, oppression of less fortunate people, bribery, corruption of innocents, wrong counsel, prostitution, all involvement with pornographic books, films, etc fornication, filthiness of spirit and of the flesh, free love, all perverted sexual acts, permissiveness and promiscuity.

GOD OUR FATHER, I apologise for the unbelievers, and sins committed through lack of faith, and for any cursing against priests or the Church in any way. I apologise for all involvement in false religions and heresies, freemasonary, spiritualism, covetousness, idolatry, charms, arrogance and deception.

GOD OUR FATHER, I ask that all children miscarried or aborted and therefore not baptised, be baptised. Amen.

GOD OUR FATHER, I apologise for all sins of involvement in New Age, reflexology, reiki healing, yoga, silva mind control, bio-energy, the enneagram, visualisation, shiatsu, aromatherapy and all other new age practices and involvements, all of which are incompatible with You, our God.

GOD OUR FATHER, I apologise for all deceit, domination, aggression, impatience, manipulation, brain washing, lack of concentration and futile dreaming.

Heavenly Father, I come before You as Your child, in great need of your help. I have physical health needs, emotional needs, spiritual needs, and interpersonal needs. Many of my problems have been caused by my own failures, neglect and sinfulness, for which I humbly beg your forgiveness, Lord. But I also ask you to forgive the sins of my ancestors whose failures have left their effects on me in the form of unwanted tendencies, behaviour patterns, moods, depression and defects in the body, mind and spirit. Heal me, Lord, of all these disorders.

With your help I sincerely forgive everyone, especially living or dead members of my family tree, who have directly offended me or my loved ones in any way, or those whose sins have resulted in our present sufferings and disorders. In the name of your divine Son, Jesus, and in the power of His Holy Spirit, I ask you Father, to deliver me and my entire family tree, including those in adoptive relationships, and those in extended family relationships, from every contaminating form of bondage. By your loving concern for us, Heavenly Father, and by the shed blood of your precious Son, Jesus, I beg you to extend your blessing to me and to all my living and deceased relatives. Heal every negative effect transmitted through all past generations, and prevent such negative effects in future generations of my family tree.

I symbolically place the cross of Jesus over the head of each person in my family tree, and between each generation; I ask you to let the cleansing blood of Jesus purify the bloodlines in my family lineage. Set your protective angels to encamp around us, and permit Archangel Raphael, the patron of healing, to administer your divine healing power to all of us, even in areas of genetic disability. Give special power to our family members' guardian angels to heal, protect, guide and encourage each of us in all our needs. Let your healing power be released at this very moment, and let it continue as long as your sovereignty permits.

In our family tree, Lord, replace all bondage with a holy bonding in family love and let there be an ever-deeper bonding with you, Lord, by the Holy Spirit, to your Son, Jesus. Let the family of the Holy Trinity pervade our family with its' tender, warm, loving presence, so that our family may recognise and manifest that love in all our relationships. All of our unknown needs we include with this petition that we pray in Jesus' precious Name. Amen.

St. Joseph, patron of family life, pray for us

Suggested Programme for a Deliverance Ceremony
Arrange for a priest to offer up a regular Mass for the specific intention.

Include the Prayer to St Michael the Archangel (full or short version) and
Prayer of Protection for Freedom from Curses & Evil
Sprinkle Holy Water & Blessed Salt

If you wish, you can also include some or all of the following prayers.
Healing of Ancestry – A Prayer of Deliverance
Apology to God Our Father or the
Prayer of Forgiveness

Suggested Programme for a Family Tree Healing Mass
Arrange for a priest to offer up a regular Mass for the specific intention.
Sprinkle Holy Water & Blessed Salt .

Include some or all of the following prayers.
Healing of Ancestry – A Prayer of Deliverance
Apology to God Our Father and the first two verses from the Prayer of Forgiveness

Summary – What can we do to stop Evil in the World

Starting with ourselves
Watch what you:
Say (your language, curses, blasphemies, negative talk against others etc)
Do (bad actions against another)
Feel (jealously, resentment, bitterness against others)
Think (be aware of negative thoughts)

Say prayers of protection on a daily basis
Wear sacramentals, a blessed cross, medals or scapular

Bless yourself with Holy Water & Blessed Salt daily - I have heard of some people put it in their food when cooking!

Become open and aware (but not paranoid) to unusual situations – especially where there are coincidences of things constantly going wrong or don't make sense.

Home and Family
Have a family tree mass celebrated to clear anything down your generations, and have the priest bless your home, car, land and family with Holy Water & Blessed Salt

Arrange for your house to be blessed or have a home enthronement to consecrate your home & family to the Two Hearts of Jesus and Mary for protection.

In Your Community
Watch out for coincidences or accumulating tragedies in your area, eg accidents, problems, bad atmosphere in an area/town.

Seek advice from someone in a prayer group who has the gift of discernment first. Arrange for masses of atonement/prayers/novenas to be celebrated, if required.

When speaking to your local priests encourage them to become aware of praying for protection for your local community/town. Maybe have your town consecrated, arrange for a deliverance ceremony for past atrocities and people currently involved in evil practices in your area.

Where do I find a person 'with discernment' who can tell me if there is something up?

Contact your local prayer group. Usually in a charismatic prayer group, there will be someone who will have a charism of the Holy Spirit and might be able to help or know someone else who can help. Check with your local priest or at http://www.charismaticrenewal.ie/index.php/prayer-groups where some groups are listed.

Where do I find a priest who can clear curses/evil?

Through my prayer life, I am familiar with a few priests and lay people in the deliverance ministry in different parts of Ireland and the UK. Currently there isn't a formal system in Ireland for dealing with deliverance. Most priests (through no fault of their own), wouldn't know what to do as it's not part of the teaching in the seminary. Again, speak to someone in a local prayer group, who might be able to direct you.

Where do I find a priest who can celebrate a Family Tree Healing Mass?

Pallotine Fathers, Thurles, Co Tipperary. 0504 21202
On Request

Saint John the Apostle, Knocknacarra, Co Galway. 091-590059
One Sunday a month

Fr Thady Doyle, Shillelagh, Co Wicklow 053 9429926
On Request

Home Enthronements
Enthronement of Homes to the Sacred Heart of Jesus and the Immaculate Heart of Mary
North – Ann 028-82246973
South – Christina 021-4667152 / Nessa 026-42185
East –   Joan 01-8255438
West –   Mary 094-9026358
Midlands – Donal 086 8172129

Acknowledgements

I would like to thank all those who took the time to supply their testimonies, provided prayers, helped with research, their time and advice. My wife Kathleen for her endless patience and support and last but not least, my daughter Eilish for the countless hours she has put down in front of the computer and time spent in bringing this booklet to completion.

References

[1] Taken from the homily of John Paul II, during his visit to the Sanctuary of Saint Michael the Archangel on 24 May 1987.

[2] Taken from the book The Mist of Mercy, Spiritual Warfare and Purgatory by 'Anne', a lay apostle. Permission kindly granted.

[3] *Memory And Reconciliation: The Church And The Faults Of The Past*
http://www.vatican.va/roman_curia/congregations/cfaith/cti_documents/rc_con_cfaith_doc_20000307_memory-reconc-itc_en.html#

[4] *Letter "Iuvenescit Ecclesia" To The Bishops Of The Catholic Church*
Regarding the Relationship Between Hierarchical and Charismatic Gifts in the Life and the Mission of the Church
http://www.vatican.va/roman_curia/congregations/cfaith/documents/rc_con_cfaith_doc_20160516_iuvenescit-ecclesia_en.html

[5] *Letter To The Bishops Of The Catholic Church On Some Aspects Of Christian Meditation*
http://www.vatican.va/roman_curia/congregations/cfaith/documents/rc_con_cfaith_doc_19891015_meditazione-cristiana_en.html

Websites

www.vatican.va
www.zenit.org